Cadell

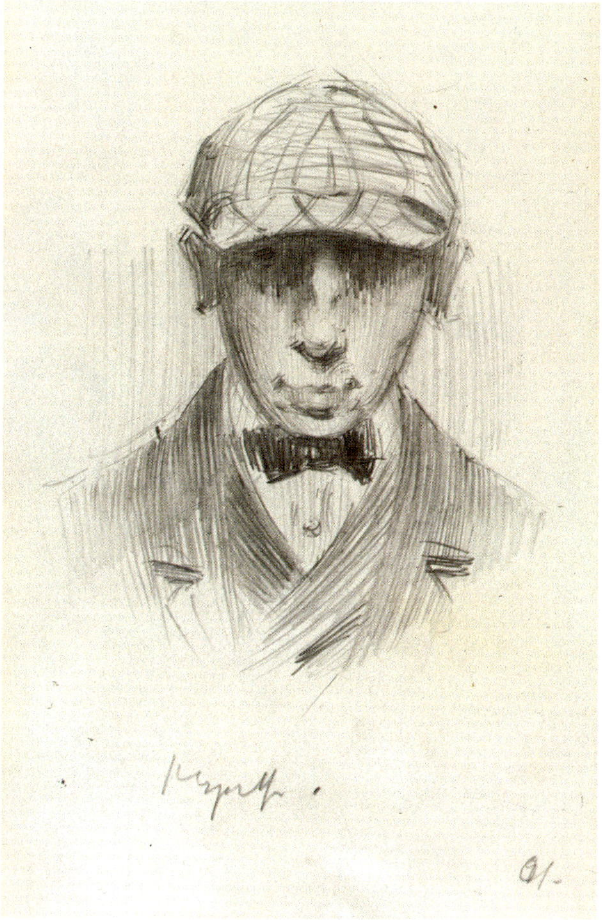

Plate 1

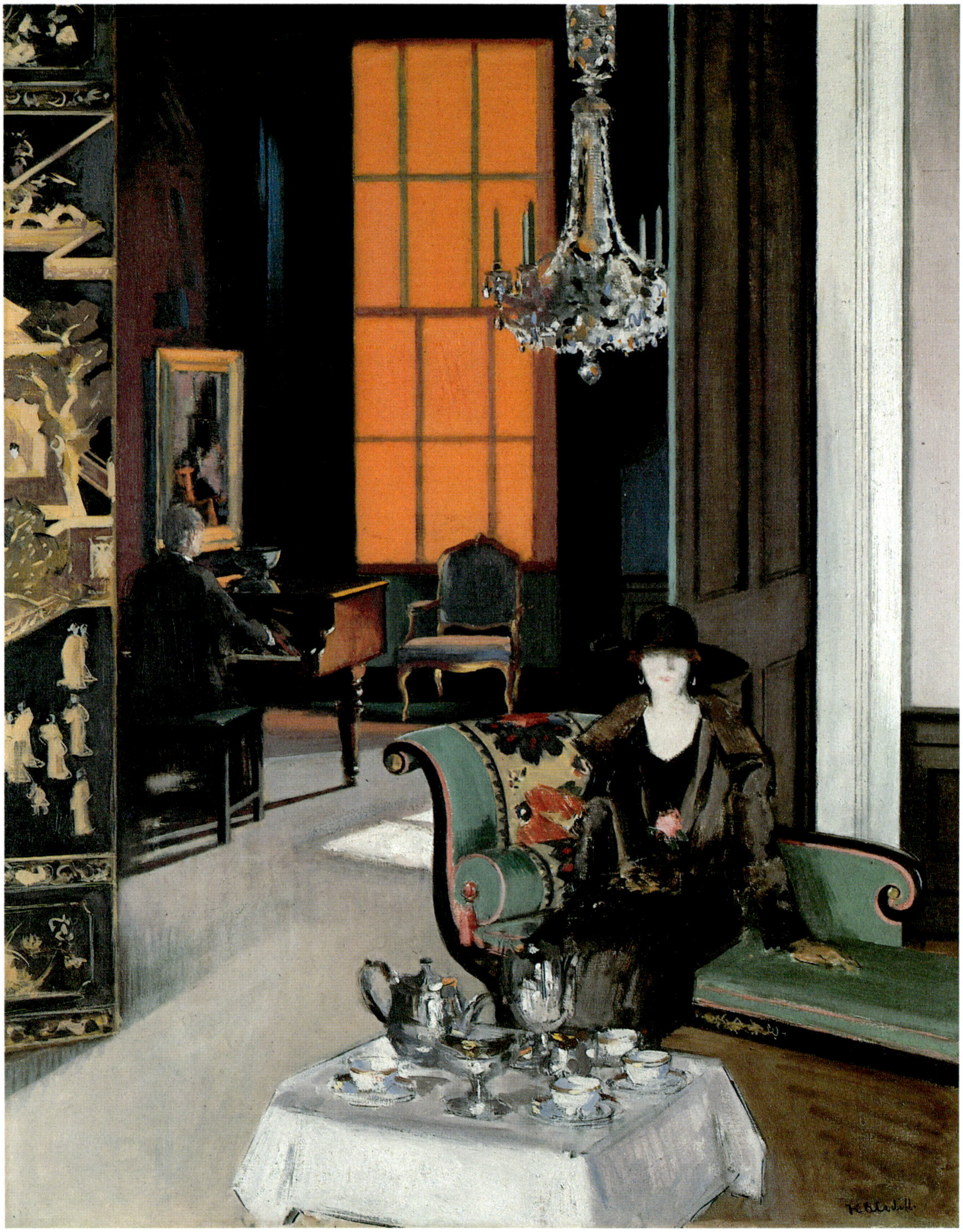

The Orange Blind, c. 1927 oil 44 × 34 in.

Cadell

The Life and Works of a Scottish Colourist 1883 – 1937

TOM HEWLETT

CANONGATE BOOKS • EDINBURGH

PORTLAND GALLERY • LONDON

First published 1988 by
THE PORTLAND GALLERY
9 Bury Street
St James's
London SW1Y 6AB
0171-321-0422
in association with
BOURNE FINE ART
4 Dundas Street
Edinburgh

This paperback edition published 1996 by
CANONGATE BOOKS
14 High Street
Edinburgh EH1 1TE
in association with
THE PORTLAND GALLERY

ISBN 0 86241 581 0

The publisher acknowledges subsidy from the
Scottish Arts Council towards publication of this book.

British Library Cataloguing-in-Publication Data
A catalogue record for this title is available
upon request from the British Library

Printed and bound in Kranj, Slovenia by Gorenjski Tisk

Contents

Foreword

Cadell, one of the most dashing of Scottish colourists, was even from his earliest Edinburgh childhood a virtuoso draughtsman and one who was almost wickedly clever with his paint brush. Some artists struggle to suppress their dexterity – Constable comes immediately to mind – so that they can retain and express greater freshness of vision. Cadell tried to do this, and confessed that he enjoyed the gentlemanly 'amateurishness' which he always detected in Gainsborough. Of all 18th century British artists this quality is hard to find in Gainsborough, but one knows what Cadell was thinking about. For me it is much more apparent in Reynolds.

Even though the artist had a very hard Great War, largely in the trenches in France, first as a Private and only latterly commissioned officer, when he was wounded, none of the associated horrors are apparent from his work. Where are the Wadsworth, Nevinson, Wyndham Lewis influences here? Weapons, barbed wire, exploding shells and the wretchedness of humanity struck no chord with the artist; nor did Dadaism, Surrealism, Cubism, that influenced so many of his contemporaries. He was a comfortable post Post-Impressionist who enjoyed warm days in Iona with blue skies and blue seas. He also relished interiors with brilliantly effulgent furniture carefully arranged and foiled against his pale mauve walls. With his fellow Colourists he responded happily and freshly to contrived still life pictures with fruit, with flowers, with jug or teapot.

His female nudes are cool and tactile, and their juxtaposition amongst familiar objects in interiors only heightens their nakedness, transforming them into mildly sensuous images. What a world they are away from Sickert's robust forms of much the same date, that also grow from the same French tradition!

Perhaps my own particular favourites are his stylish portraits of women in black hats. Here we have the compositional dexterity of a Singer Sargent or a de Lazlo but, rather than being flattering, particularised portraits they have become transformed into memorable images of supremely modish Edwardian women. In Cadell his canvases do not disturb the psyche or particularly intrigue the intellect, but they are joyous, brilliantly coloured simple statements that delight in structural composition, and painterly facture. His character fitted his art.

As my predecessor Stanley Cursiter commented:

"Cadell was spontaneous and gay; for him nature in her brightest dress was the reflection of his own joy in the paints on his palette".

Timothy Clifford, Director of the National Galleries of Scotland
Edinburgh August 1988.

Plate 2

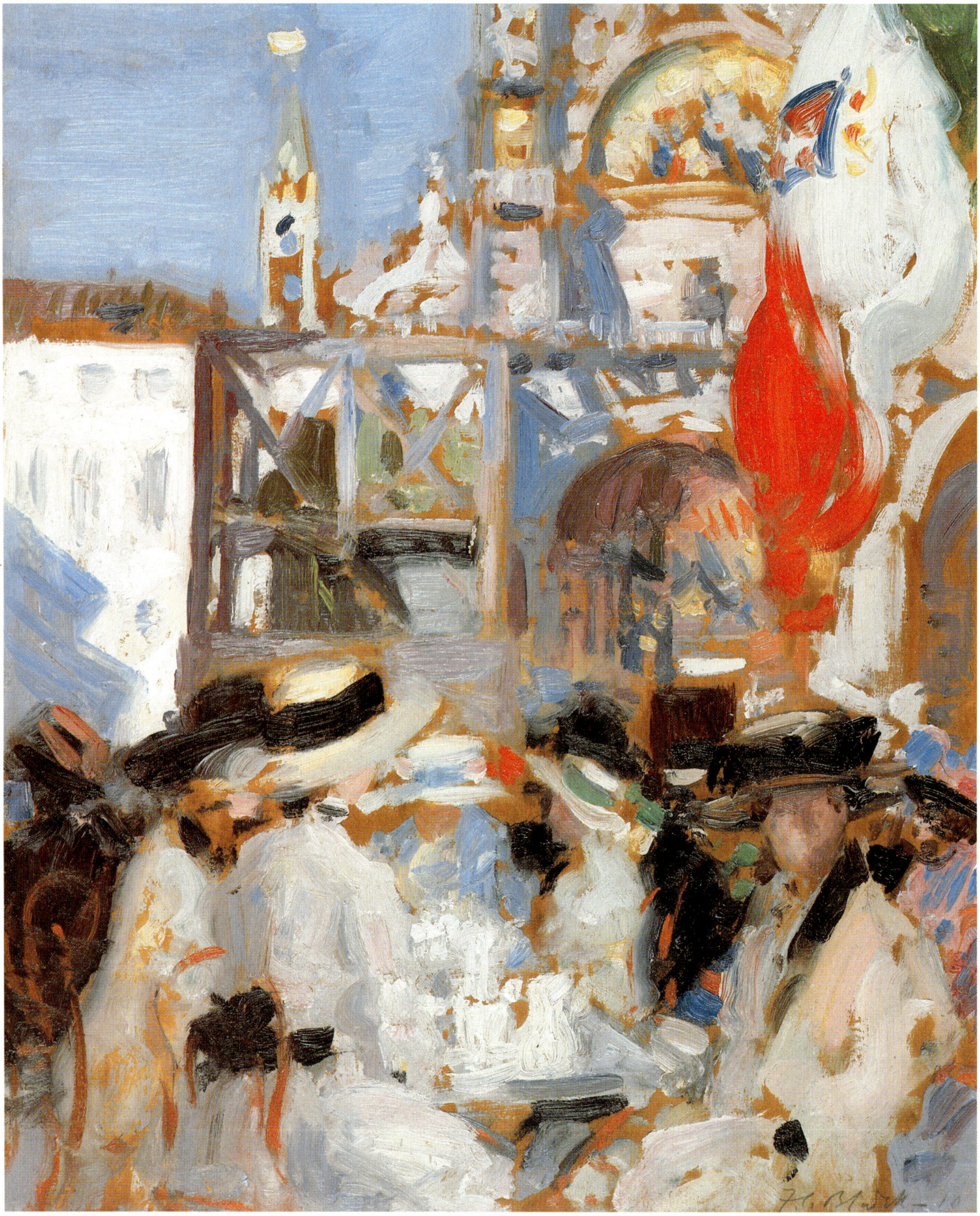

Florian's Café, Venice, 1910 oil 18 × 15 in.

Acknowledgments

My grateful thanks to the numerous private collectors who have allowed me into their homes to see their Cadell paintings, and, in many cases to give me information and anecdotes about the artist.

I would also like to record my sincere thanks to those whose help has made this book possible – Mr and Mrs John Cadell, Simon Cadell, Patrick Cadell and other members of the artist's family; Timothy Clifford, Director of the National Galleries of Scotland; Bill Smith of Robert Fleming Holdings Ltd.; Iain Harrison, Guy Peploe, Patrick Bourne, Joanna Shipp, Paul Harris, and Roy Fox of Rodney Todd-White; the Royal Scottish Academy, the Royal Glasgow Institute and the Royal Scottish Society of Painters in Watercolour.

I would like to thank my wife and four young children for putting up with a sometimes absent and over-occupied husband and father.

Tom Hewlett
London August 1988.

Most of the illustrations in this book have been made possible by the kind consent of private collectors who have asked to remain anonymous. Works not in private collections are as follows:

Interior Salute, Venice (Plate 17) Alex. Reid & Lefevre Ltd.
Afternoon (Plate 26) Courtesy Sotheby's Ltd.
Florian's Café, Venice (Plate 2) Portland Gallery
Crème de Menthe (Plate 39) McLean Museum and Art Gallery
Reflections (Plate 42) Glasgow Art Gallery and Museum
Peggy in Black and Pink (Plate 38) Courtesy Sotheby's Ltd.
Cassis (Plate 58) Royal Bank of Scotland PLC
A Lady in Black (Plate 63) Glasgow Art Gallery and Museum
The Gold Chair (Plate 48) Portland Gallery
The Blue Room (Plate 84) Portland Gallery
Arum Lillies (Plate 47) Alex. Reid & Lefevre Ltd.
The Negro (Plate 55) Courtesy Sotheby's Ltd.
The Dunara Castle (Plate 65) Robert Fleming Holdings Ltd.
The Orange Blind (Plate 1) Glasgow Art Gallery and Museum
The Poet (Plate 91) Royal Scottish Academy
Loch Creran, Argyll (Plate 80) Robert Fleming Holdings Ltd.
Roses (Plate 43) Robert Fleming Holdings Ltd.

Introduction

In his introduction to the Cadell Memorial Exhibition held at Glasgow Art Gallery in June 1942, Stanley Cursiter wrote:

"But no appreciation of his art is adequate without a note on the man . . . He was of middle height and robust build, he walked with a certain jauntiness of step – a straight and serviceable pipe gripped firmly in his teeth, an eye that lifted to a twinkle and a smile ready to expand to a quick laugh; careful in dress but seldom without a gay, distinctive note – shepherd tartan trousers – a blue scarf – a yellow waistcoat – or all the glory of his kilt, but with all – an air! Indeed, it needs little imagination to see him in the costume of the eighteenth century or of the seventeenth century in France, or at any period when wit could be a passport to the highest grace. His wit was constant and brilliant – caustic, sardonic, Rabelasian, or lightly bantering – it was but an indication of many sided accomplishment which found expression in colour, in verse and in life itself."

Cursiter's tribute, together with an extract from a letter that Cadell wrote to one of his patrons in 1933, gives the key to why he is now properly regarded as one of the foremost of twentieth century Scottish artists. Cadell wrote:

"He (Whistler) was a marvellous painter – the most exquisite of the 'moderns', and he had what some great painters have – a certain 'amateurishness' which I rather like and feel always in Gainsborough. I can best describe what I mean in these words. 'A gentleman painting for his amusement', (of course it must be understood that the said 'gentleman' is a genius as well!) . . . this quality or defect (whichever you like to call it in great painters) is exceedingly rare".

The same letter could be written, substituting Cadell's name for that of Whistler, and be equally valid. He was born with natural artistic ability and a deep desire to express his love of life through his work.

Cadell is now primarily thought of as a 'Colourist' and his work is bracketed together with that of the other three Scottish Colourists, S. J. Peploe, (1871-1935), J. D. Fergusson (1874-1961) and Leslie Hunter (1877-1931).

However, the title 'Colourist' deserves some explanation as there are many examples of the use of bold colour in Scottish painting before the emergence of these four artists. William MacTaggart (1835–1910), widely regarded as 'The Father of Scottish Impressionism' pioneered the use of a lighter and brighter palette. Similarly, members of the Glasgow School, particularly W. Y. Macgregor (1855-1923), James Guthrie (1859-1930), George Henry (1858-1943), E. A. Hornel (1864-1933), and Arthur Melville (1855-1904) regularly demonstrated their enthusiasm for the use of strong, fresh colours and subtle tonal contrasts.

There is no doubt that both the work of the Glasgow School artists, and the artists themselves, had an effect on the early careers of the Colourists. Fergusson wrote:

"Although I never met him (Melville) or saw him, his paintings gave me my first start; his work opened up to me the road to freedom – not merely freedom in the use of paint, but freedom of outlook."

As we shall see, Melville had a more direct impact on Cadell's career by encouraging his parents to allow him to go to Paris at the age of 16, to study painting.

Apart from the official tuition that he received between 1899 and 1902, the exposure to the powerful forces that were emerging in France at the time and during his subsequent return visits to Paris obviously had an effect on the young artist. He would clearly have seen the Fauve works of Matisse and Derain, for example. The influence of the work of the Impressionists, which could be seen at Durand Ruel's Gallery and at Salle Caillebotte, was particularly strong and some of Cadell's best early work (Plates 14 & 89) emphasises the mark that these paintings made on him.

However, there is nothing in his work pre 1910, except perhaps his small oil *'Assembly Rooms'* (Plate 12), to give any indication of the explosion of colour that was to take place in some of his 1910 Venetian paintings (Plates 2 & 19). Not all the work that he produced during his visit was in the same vivid high key, indeed many of the works (Plates 17 & 18) show little development in terms of tone and colour from the small oil panel *'French Farm'*, 1907, (Plate 7), and the watercolours executed at Grange in 1908 (Plates 9 & 11). But those few oils that displayed the spontaneous use of bold, bright colour were sufficient to signal the arrival of a new and highly individual 'Colourist' talent.

The Venice paintings were exhibited in Edinburgh in the autumn of 1910, just prior to Roger Fry's first Post Impressionist Exhibition at the Grafton Gallery in London.

While Peploe and Fergusson spent most of their time in the pre-war years in France, Cadell remained in Scotland, mainly in Edinburgh. Having led a fairly nomadic existence for the previous ten years there was clearly an attraction in having a permanent base from which to operate. Financial considerations were also important, as friends and patrons were largely from Edinburgh.

The result was that Cadell had little, if any, direct contact with progressive ideas about art that emanated from Europe generally, and Paris in particular, after about 1910. What contact he did have was mainly through his close friendship with Peploe.

Instead, he concentrated on the subject matter that was at hand. To understand how he found sufficient challenging material in the relative confines of Edinburgh during autumn and spring, and Iona in the summer, (he rarely painted during the winter), one *must* understand his character, for the work and the person were inextricably linked.

Above all, Cadell was an optimist, who had no interest in the less savoury elements of life. He saw beauty in many forms and was devoted to using his extraordinary artistic versatility to convey that beauty to others. As Guy Peploe wrote in his Critical Memoir:

"The almost complete lack of 'angst' in his work seems to derive from an intense love of life, a sensuous enjoyment of good living and an admiration for men who were masculine and women who were elegant. His subject-matter reflected his hedonism. Whether he was painting landscape, still life, interiors or figures, there was in it a glow of health and beauty."

Pre-war Edwardian Edinburgh provided a wealth of elegant subject matter for Cadell. Plates 20 and 25 show the beginning of his particular technique of using the shimmer of reflected colour to heighten the richness of a painting. Yet his work of this period seems

Plate 3

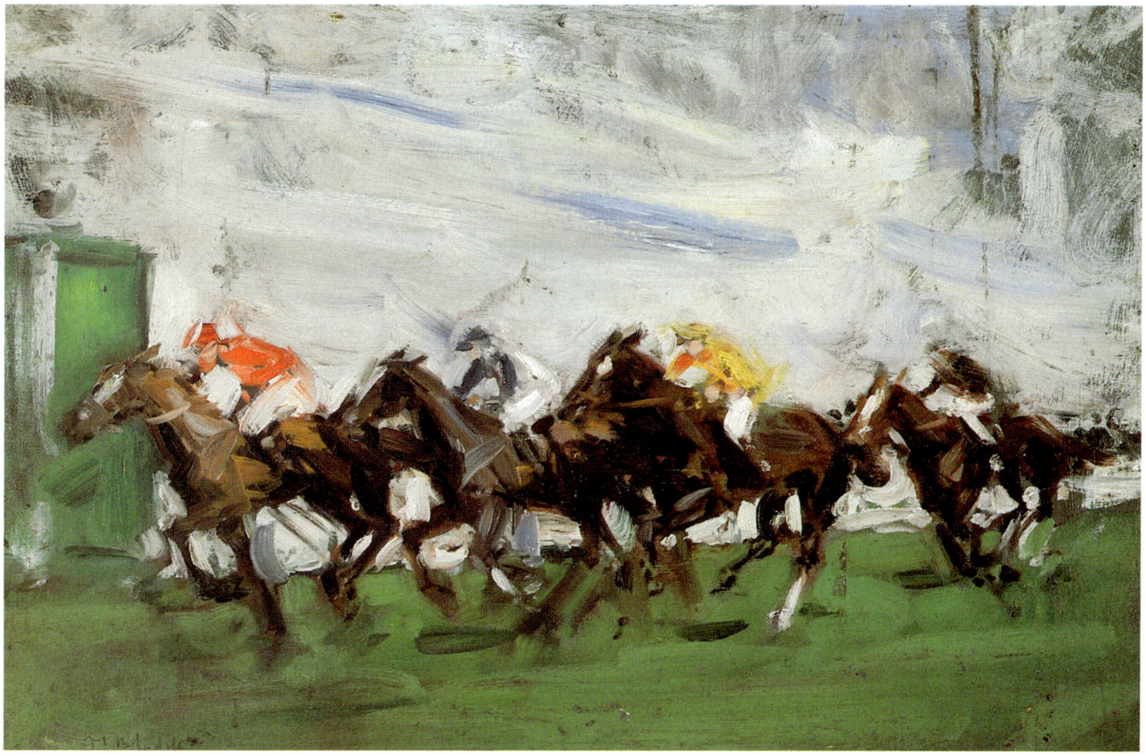

The Finish oil 12 × 18 in.

more a development of his impressionist inspired paintings of 1908 and 1909 than of his high keyed Venetian ones. The predominant colour is often a rich, creamy white, with occasional splashes of pastel green, blue and orange. To heighten the contrast and give the impression of space and light, Cadell would sometimes make the focal point of the painting a darker coloured object, (the interiors regularly featuring a fashionable black hat). *'Afternoon'*, 1913 (Plate 26) is one of the first examples of his use of a highly polished black wooden floor to achieve this contrast.

A regular summer visitor to Iona after 1912, his early landscapes of the island use the same range of colours as his pre-war interiors. It was not until after the war that Cadell painted on unprimed board to impart a chalky consistency and almost luminous quality to his work (Plate 62). Whenever he did this he inscribed a warning on the back of the painting 'Absorbent ground, *NEVER* varnish'. He was meticulous in giving a title to almost every painting but works were rarely dated after 1913.

The most dramatic change in the style of Cadell's work came after the end of the war. Perhaps in a reaction to the squalor and chaos of the trenches, his still life and interior works took on a completely new form. Pure primary colours in a deliberate and well defined structure replaced the looser handling and spontaneity of the pre-war paintings. It is works of this period (Plates 45 & 58) that confirm Cadell's status as a Colourist. These paintings also help to underline one of Cadell's greatest attributes – his remarkable versatility. Always working with an obvious interest in the quality of the paint, he seemed equally at home with any subject. Indeed, in his assessment of the relative strengths of Cadell, Peploe and Hunter, Ion Harrison concludes:

"Cadell certainly excelled in painting interiors in a manner which neither Peploe nor Hunter could equal. I also think that Cadell was the most versatile of the three. He painted landscapes, seascapes, figure subjects, cows, sheep, ships and boats with equal facility. One of the finest pictures of a horse race I have ever seen was a small oil painted by Cadell (Plate 3). To my mind it equalled for action, both of horses and jockeys, anything ever painted by Degas".

Towards the end of his career the angularity of his paintings of the 1920's gave way to an equally colourful but more pattern orientated approach as shown by both the portrait of Mrs Harrison (Plate 79) and *'Interior, Croft House'* (Plate 78).

However, two common characteristics can be seen running through the best of Cadell's work, irrespective of when it was painted – elegance and optimism. As Stanley Cursiter commented:

"His most valuable asset is an infective gaiety, a light-heartedness, combined with a daring and masterful use of colour – placed with a swift certainty of its effective display".

In the immediate months prior to his death it would have been easy for Cadell to have become depressed. Surrounded by unsold paintings, and suffering from a horribly painful cancer, he was forced to enter hospital. His doctors wrote to his sister of his tremendous courage but, above all, his unconscionable humour.

Cadell's obituary in the Edinburgh Academy Chronicle referred to him as a "great character, a gallant gentleman and a brilliant artist" who, "had he been spared in good health, would undoubtedly have become one of the R.S.A.'s most distinguished Presidents". Although this was only conjecture, there is no doubt that Cadell's death at the relatively young age of fifty-four deprived the Scottish art world of one of its most charismatic and talented figures.

Chapter One

1883–1908

Francis Campbell Boileau 'Bunty' Cadell was born on April 12th 1883. He was born into a family that had roots going back to the early part of the eighteenth century in and around Edinburgh. Yet there was an artistic vein that ran through the outwardly traditional family that ensured that the prodigious natural artistic talent he possessed would be nurtured and encouraged rather than stifled.

He was christened Francis (after his father), but quickly became known as 'Bunty', a particularly Scottish nickname suggesting slightly mischievous but endearing qualities. The name stayed with him throughout his life. His father was a respected Edinburgh doctor with more than a passing interest in the arts – particularly painting; (the celebrated artist Arthur Melville was godfather to the family's second son, Arthur). His mother, née Mary Hamilton Boileau, was a devoted and supportive figure whose family originally came from Nîmes, in France. The Cadells also had a daughter, Jean, the famous actress to whom Bunty remained close throughout his life.

It soon became clear that young Bunty had been blessed with a rare artistic talent. He could draw passably well by the age of three; happily, his mother kept many of her son's early works in a scrapbook which has remained with the family. Some examples from it are illustrated (Plates 4 & 5).

What was not clear at this time but soon became so, was that Bunty possessed much more than mere ability as an artist. He also had the natural gift of injecting life and good humour into almost any situation. He had a quick wit and generous soul and neither deserted him during his life. They helped make him very much the centre of any gathering and ensured that his company was often in demand. This proved to be of welcome assistance in the many financially lean years that were to follow.

Formal education at Edinburgh Academy Preparatory School was uneventful and uninspiring. Written in 1893, the 'General Conduct' section of Bunty's second school report indicates his main interest.

"He makes more effort to give his attention to his work though little sketches are still produced at intervals, – a pencil in his hand at any time is dangerous to lessons."

His request to be allowed to concentrate on the artistic side of his education received support from his parents. However, his early experience at art school in Edinburgh did not provide him with the inspiration that he sought. Indeed, his most impressive works of this period are caricatures of the teaching staff. Similarly, his subsequent studies at the Royal Scottish Academy Life School are best remembered for a well known story that Bunty often told when anyone asked him why he painted left handed. According to the story, Bunty was addressed by the President of the R.S.A. Life School who remarked that no artist had ever become successful painting left handed. His reply was quick and sure. "Sir, did not Michaelangelo paint with his left hand?" At a loss for words, the President departed leaving a fellow student to ask his friend how he knew that Michaelangelo was left handed. The inevitable reply came back – "I didn't know, but nor did the President."

Plate 4

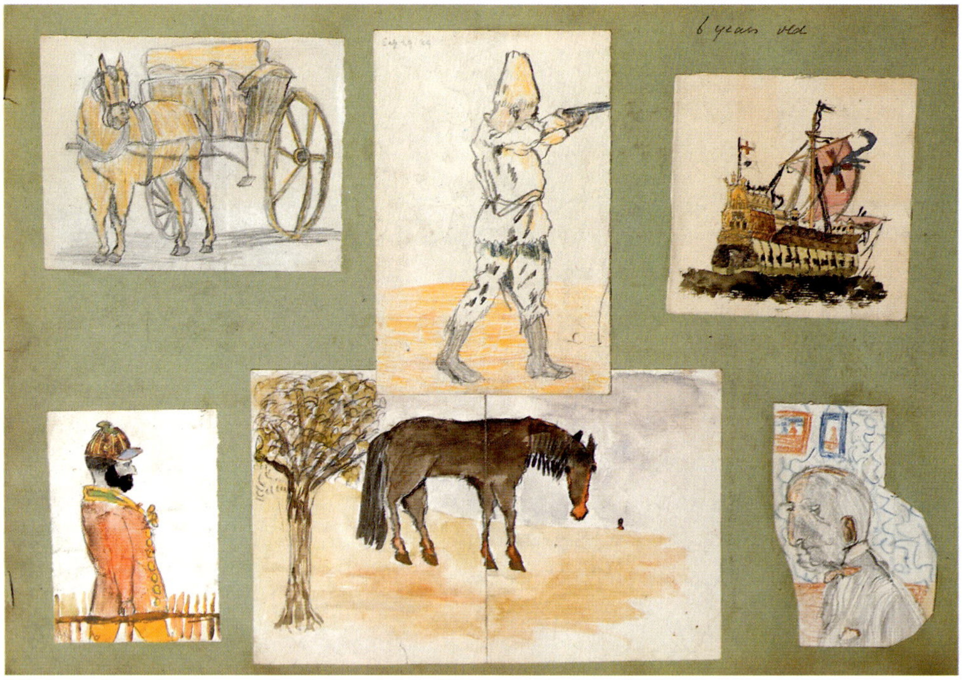

Scrapbook, 1889

Bunty was soon disillusioned with Edinburgh's traditional ways of teaching art. His natural ability as a draughtsman made the theory and discussion about technique more a frustration than a help. This became obvious to his parents who turned to their close friend Arthur Melville for advice. Melville, himself a highly talented and individual artist – and leading light of the Glasgow School – had no hesitation in recommending a dramatic solution to the problem. Aware of the breadth of vision in artistic circles in France generally, and Paris in particular, he suggested that young Cadell should study there. It was not something for which the family had planned, but it was further evidence of his parents' commitment that in 1899, at the age of 16, Bunty travelled to Paris with his mother and sister to begin three years of training at Academie Julien (where Peploe had also studied) and some of the other most respected studios in Paris.

It was not long before Bunty became aware that the rather traditional style of painting that he was employing at the time was not going to excite the Paris public. In a letter to his father in 1900 he wrote,

"None of my watercolours have sold yet and I don't expect they will over here, they would be much more likely to sell at home. I have just finished a very good watercolour portrait of myself, (Plate 6), which I may send to the S.S.A."

Life in the French capital was not that easy, but it did have its lighter moments as Bunty reported back to his father in his typically amusing way.

Plate 5

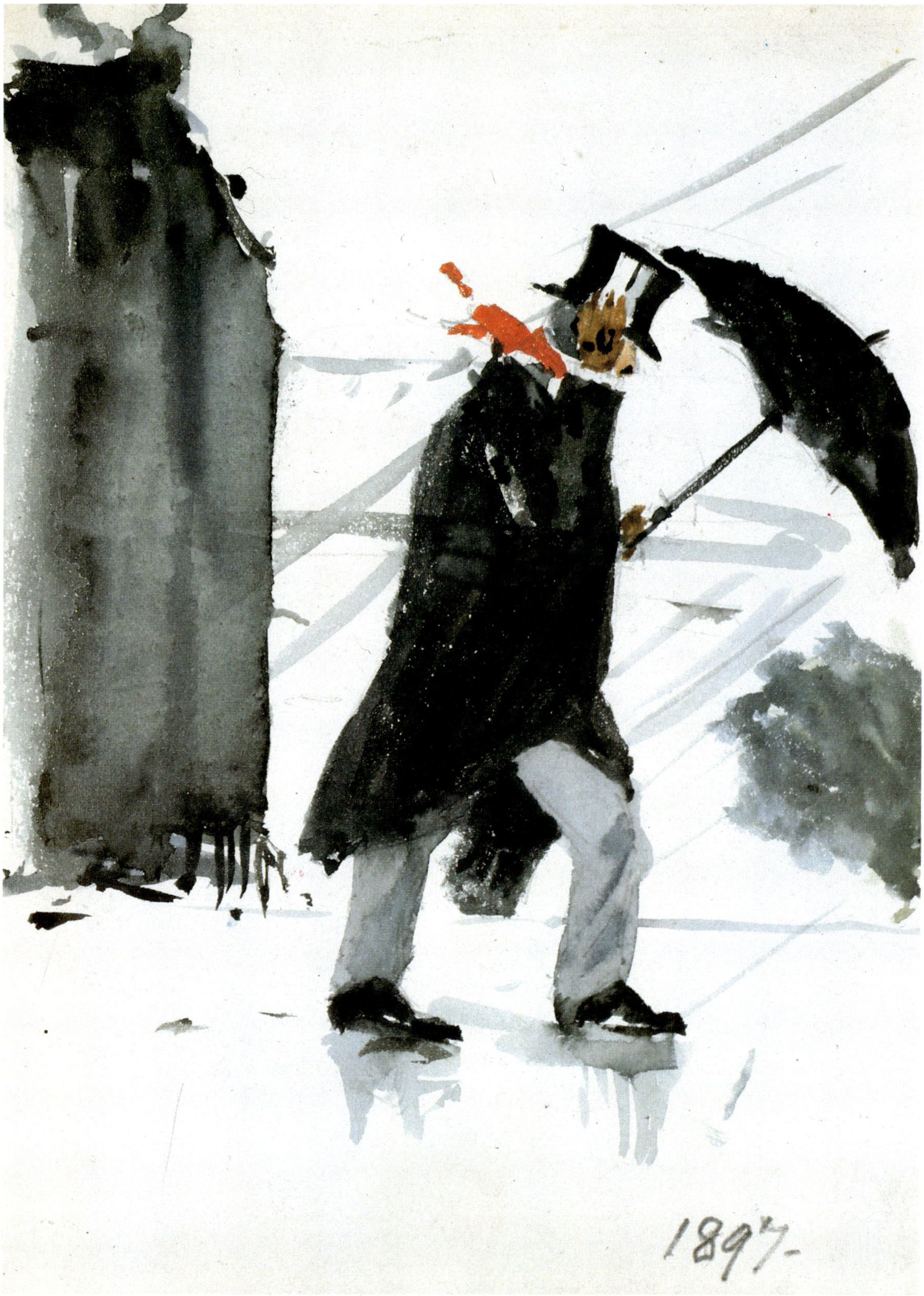

Scrapbook, 1897

Plate 6

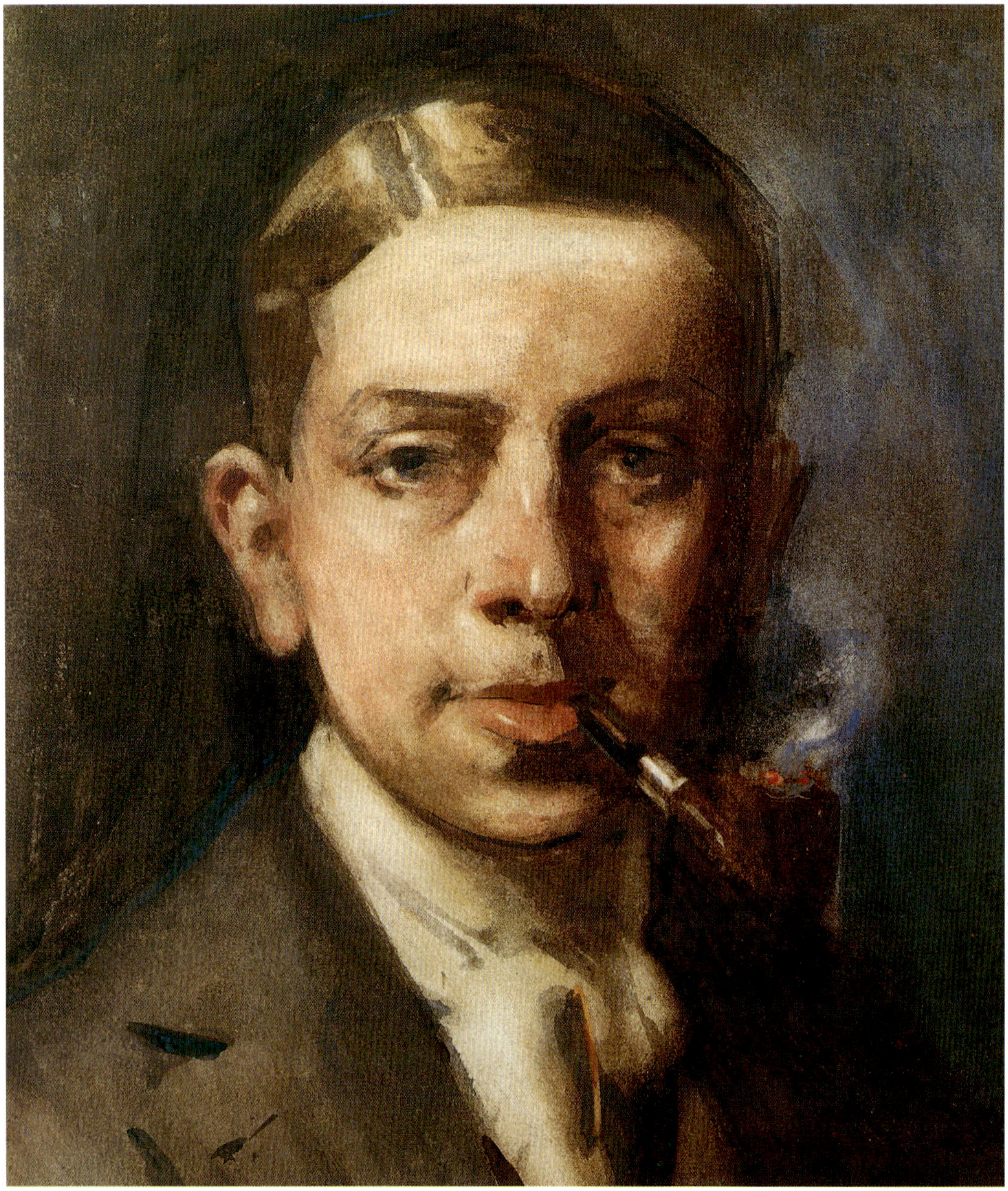

Self-portrait, 1900 watercolour 15 × 11 in.

"I sat next to a duke at dinner. He talked to me all the time except when I saw an opportunity to turn him off onto (the lady) who sat on his right. For whenever he talked he spat pieces of his dinner into my plate and dropped beads of perspiration into his own!"

There is little doubt that Paris had an immediate and marked influence on the young artist. He thrived on the less rigid and more colourful approach to art; the vitality excited him. He had a small watercolour exhibited in the Paris Salon in 1899. The work that he started to produce at this time and in the immediate aftermath of his training in Paris showed a distinct impressionist influence with the tendency to exaggerate colour. 1902 saw his first paintings exhibited at the Royal Scottish Academy; there was a Parisian landscape – '*Notre Dame from the Seine*', and a portrait. Three paintings were also exhibited at the Society of Scottish Artists (S.S.A.).

Although Bunty's early studies in Paris ended in 1903, he returned to France on numerous occasions throughout the first part of his life. In both 1905 and 1906 he sold works at the New Salon; both were still life paintings on panel and sold for twelve pounds and twelve guineas respectively. They were the first still lifes that Bunty sold, and were wholly different in subject matter from the 'stock in trade' landscape and portrait works that he had been selling in Scotland at the same time. They were clearly the forerunners of some of his most successful later works.

Back in Scotland, and before moving to Munich with his family late in 1906, Bunty found it difficult to derive any meaningful income from his painting. He was based at the family home in Edinburgh but made regular trips out of town to stay with friends, particularly in Galloway and Dumfriesshire. One of his favourite haunts was Shambellie House, then home of the Stewart family, but since donated to the National Museums of Scotland as a Museum of Costume. Bunty's introduction to the house was made through a young Edinburgh friend, and legal student, C. E. (Ted) Stewart whose father, William, owned the estate. Bunty's friendship with Ted Stewart was to last his lifetime; Ted was a regular patron of Bunty from an early stage and acquired his first painting, a watercolour entitled '*Sweetheart Abbey*', in 1907. He also became the secretary of the Society of Eight when it was founded in 1912, and executor of Bunty's estate in 1938.

Bunty treated Shambellie very much as a second home. He returned frequently to stay with the family, being affectionately known as 'Uncle Bunty' by the young Stewarts and their friends who met him there. This was indicative of the special rapport that he instantly seemed to create with children. Although he never married, he was able to establish an unusual camaraderie and loyalty with the youngsters that he met; they were enchanted by him and his marvellous ability to make life fun. One of his favourite games was to invent mythical characters, many of which still remain vivid in the minds of those for whom they were created. More than fifty years later someone who, as a child, met Bunty, wrote:

"He used to entertain me with tales of a highly eccentric and imaginary female called Aunt Crack. She was an elderly spinster with a very long, sharp nose, rather like some of the frumps he drew for Jack and Tommy. The nose was adorned with pince-nez, chained to her bosom, and for ear-rings she wore on one side a bird cage with a parrot in it and on the other a gun carriage; she also had a taste for large and extraordinary hats.

I remember her well because one or two of his drawings of her were framed and hung on my nursery wall. Unhappily they disappeared when my parents sold the house in 1930 . . . I don't know if Crack was invented for my benefit or if Uncle Bunty used her to charm other children of his acquaintance. If so, there may still be treasured drawings of her in other families. It would be wonderful if she turned up. I would so like to see her again!"

Bunty was also fond of composing occasional lines of verse. On one visit to Shambellie, he wrote a poem about the house; the children staying at the time were each asked to learn some verses. The poem which was titled 'The Bloated Grange', was then performed in front of the adults before dinner with each child reciting his allotted verses and then all joining in the chorus. It ran as follows:

"Beware! Beware the kitchen stair,
For there the goblins make their lair.
The ghosts you meet will raise your hair.
        Beware! Beware!
For Jim may come and Jim may go,
But Jim-Jams you will have, I know.

There you will find the Mormon bride
Sit staring at you open-eyed
Her gruesome jaws a-gaping wide
        Oh! Woe betide!
For Jim etc.

Below the stairs a darksome den,
If you go there at half-past ten
You'll find the tattie-bogle hen
        You never ken.

I dread the wash-house I confess.
The laundry also, more or less,
But most of all, as you may guess
        The napery-press.

Here squirming on the ground there lies
A formless mass which groans and sighs,
Blue-bottles humming round its eyes
        A beauty prize!

Oh! You should see the boot hole dark
Where adders lie in pumps and bark.
You'll leave its horrors staring stark,
        Let me remark.

But far, far worse than any ghost
With whacking cough a ghastly host.
Sits tearing at our last week's roast
        The Sunday Post.

Oh, shun this spot if life is dear!
No quarter you'll discover here
Except perhaps a quart o' beer
        It's very queer.

Above the stairs the great North Wing
Where female goblins nightly sing,
Or, screaming, dance a jing-a-ring
        They're quite the thing.

And through the door a loathly tank
Within a chamber dark and dank
Still victims sink where others sank,
        And died, and stank.

Therein are monsters great and small
Who squirm and wriggle one and all,
And round and round they creep and crawl,
        Till in you fall.

Then if they catch you by the toe
They'll never, never let you go
Till they have dragged you down below,
        Oh! ho-ho-ho-! Oh! ho-ho-ho!

Down there you'll find two hollow caves
Submerged beneath the dirty waves;
In each a wretched captive raves
        And freedom craves.

There jolly fish their victims munch
And mammoth putrid bodies scrunch
Their greasy backs with greed they hunch
        Oh! What a lunch!

The owners of this clammy cell
Call it a bath, instead of hell
(There's nothing left of those who fell
        Except the smell).

Moral. Avoid this mansion strange
However much you need a change
It's full of pestilence and mange –
        A Bloated Grange."

Plate 7

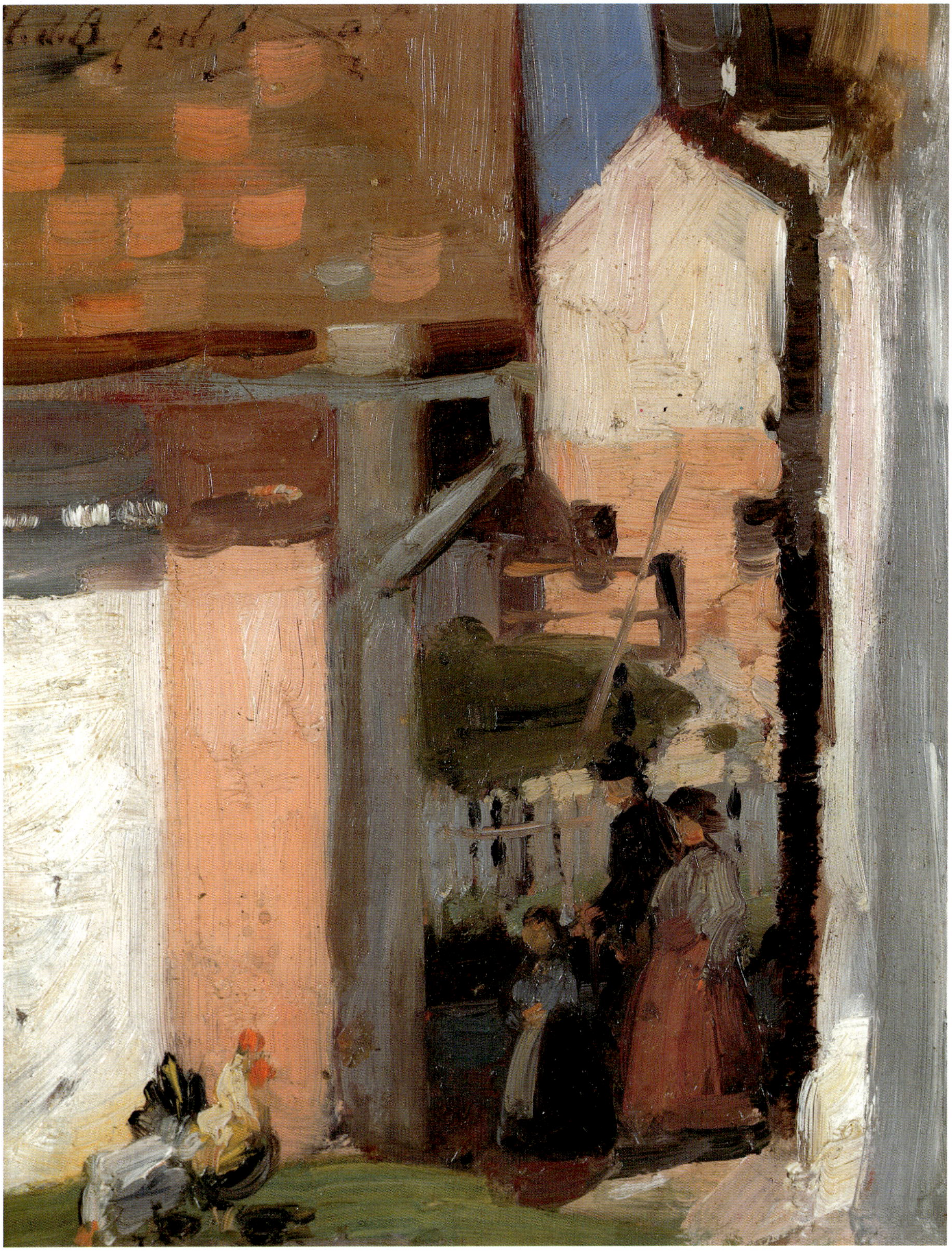

French Farm, 1907 oil 14 × 10 in.

Plate 8

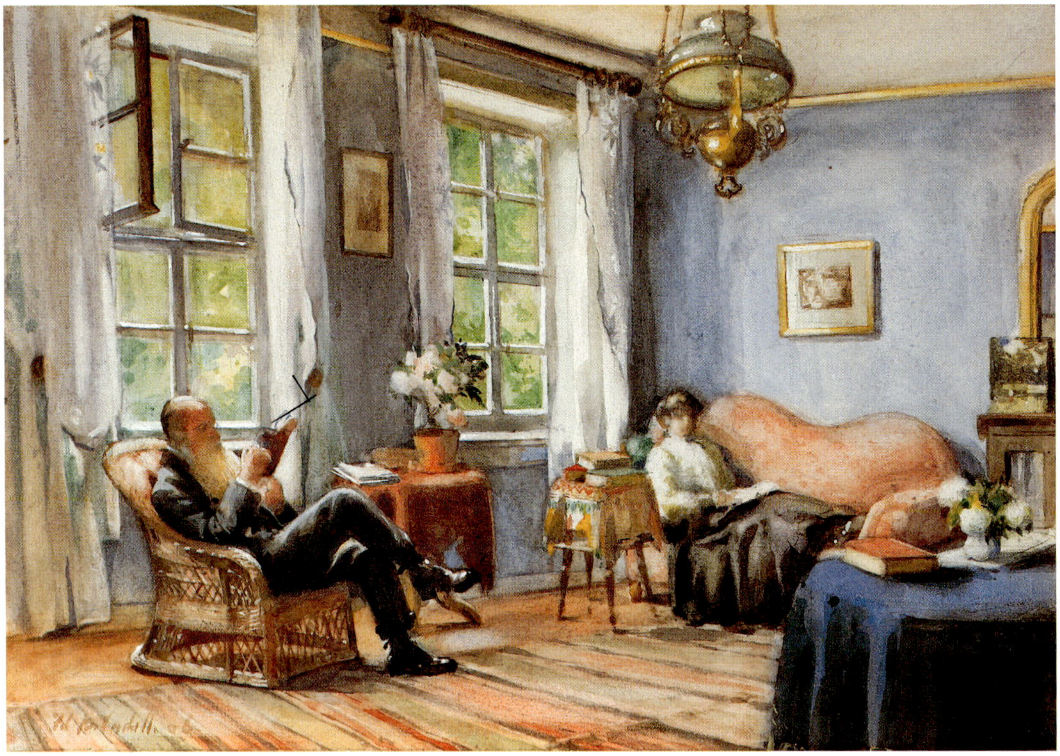

My Parents at Gotha, 1906 watercolour 10 × 14 in.

Although Bunty's early trips to Shambellie were more for social reasons than an attempt to sell his paintings, his work attracted a following from the Stewart family and some of their friends and relations. His records show that in 1903 he sold a total of five paintings for £53-11/-. Two of these were portraits of the Cliff-McCulloch family, priced at fifteeen guineas each. One was a portrait of Miss Nellie Watson, priced at ten guineas, and two were watercolours for which Bunty charged eight and three guineas respectively.

1904 saw only twenty guineas income – from another Cliff McCulloch portrait and, although 1905 saw seven paintings sold (including the still life in Paris, referred to earlier), his income from sales of paintings amounted to a meagre £55-18/-.

The next two years were no better, and Bunty was pre-occupied with other events. His father was taken ill and had to give up his lucrative medical practice in the centre of Edinburgh in 1906. Probably in an attempt to live more economically, the family moved to Munich. Bunty continued his studies, and sketched and painted extensively. The subjects that he chose were mainly landscapes and helped form the nucleus of his first exhibition in Edinburgh. However, the family's stay in Germany was cut short when Mrs Cadell died unexpectedly, and tragically. It was a cruel blow to the close knit family but particularly for Bunty who, as the eldest son, had always had a very close relationship with his mother. The family returned to Edinburgh early in 1908, but had no home to go to, having sold their house at 22 Ainslie Place the year before. Bunty left to stay with the Stewarts at Shambellie. There, he recharged his batteries and prepared for the exhibition that was held later that year

Plate 9

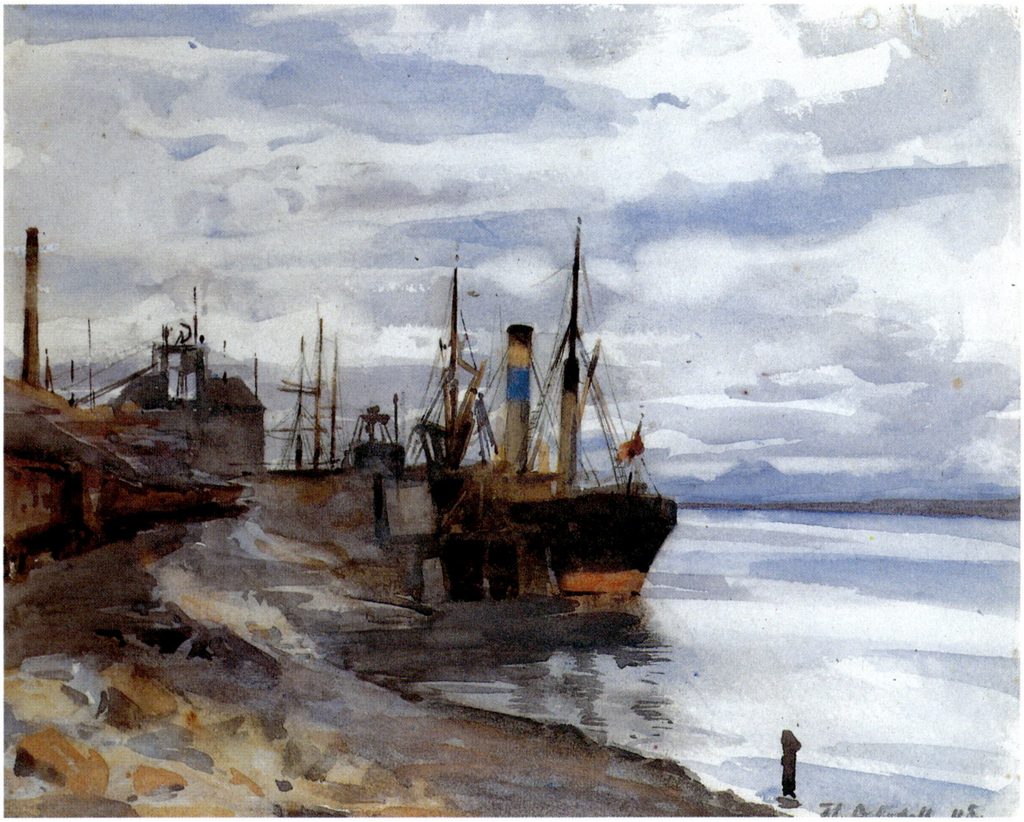

Bridgness Coal Pier, 1908 watercolour 10 × 14 in.

at Doig, Wilson & Wheatley's in Edinburgh. Before Bunty returned to the capital, the Stewarts had purchased two more paintings, one a delightful oil of the family spaniel *'Price'* who had featured in somewhat uncomplimentary fashion in verse five of 'The Bloated Grange'.

There is little doubt that Bunty's first exhibition at Doig's marked a major milestone in his career. Not only did he sell thirty paintings in the show, but he also established contact with various collectors who were to play an important and supportive role in the years that followed, none more so than his old school friend P. J. (later Sir Patrick) Ford, who purchased four works. It was the first occasion on which Bunty has sold a painting for £25 (an oil entitled *'Summer'*) and although there was a degree of support from friends and family who wanted to ensure that his first major show was successful, the exhibition was well supported by the public and by the gallery's clients who had not been exposed to Bunty's work before.

The bulk of the paintings that sold at the exhibition were landscapes (both oil and watercolour) of Scotland, Germany and Paris. None were colourist paintings as we would define them today. Yet, at the time the free, almost impressionist technique combined with the accentuated colours and tones that Bunty employed as shown in *'Assembly Rooms'*, (Plate 12), made it abundantly clear to some that a new and exciting talent had arrived.

Plate 10

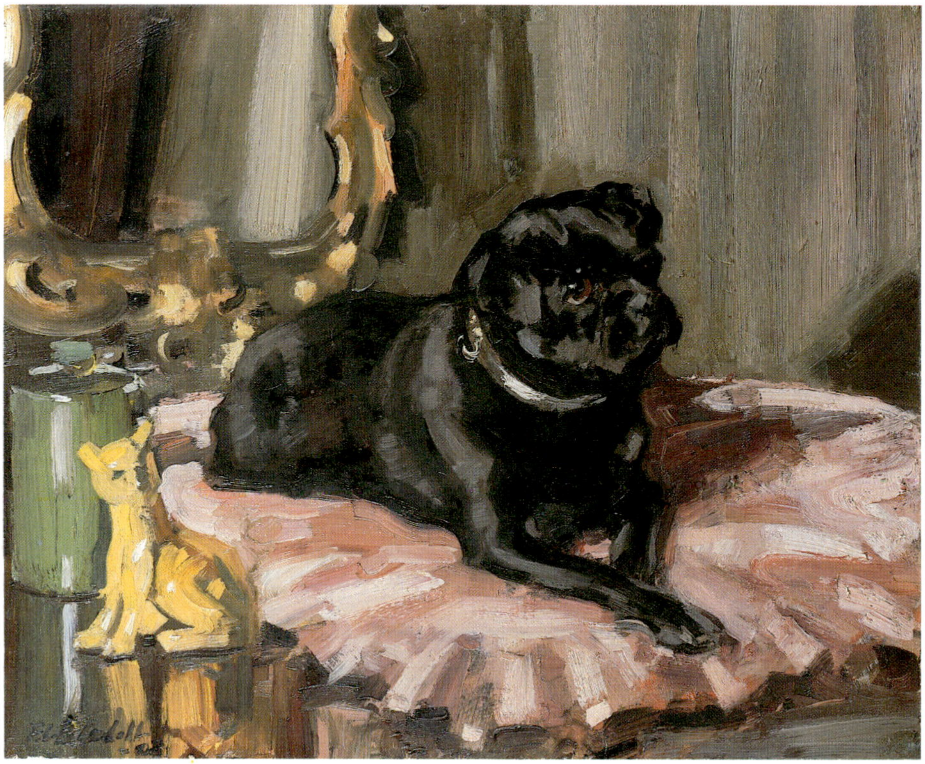

Shambellie Pug, 1908 oil 20 × 24 in.

In September, after the Doig exhibition, Bunty was invited to stay and paint at Grange, the West Lothian home of his distant relative Henry Moubray Cadell, the 'senior member' of the Cadell family. H. M. Cadell was a direct descendant of William Cadell of Cockenzie, the founder of the Carron Ironworks, whose factory had started production in the mid 1770's and later became famous not just as one of Scotland's largest employers but also for producing many of the cannons used at Waterloo, and the original cast iron post boxes.

Bunty's first stay at Grange resulted in his selling three watercolours to his relations. For '*Bridgness Coal Pier*' (Plate 9) he charged eight pounds while two watercolours of '*Garden at Grange*', sold for four pounds each. One of the latter was subsequently given away as a wedding present in 1918 and seventy years later, appeared on the television programme, 'The Antiques Road Show', where it was estimated to be worth around one thousand five hundred pounds. This watercolour (Plate 11) helps to illustrate the marvellous perspective that so many of his paintings achieved.

After another visit to Shambellie in late September, Bunty returned to Grange as a paying guest. His payment took the form of paintings of the house and its grounds, and, in addition, the family purchased three other watercolours.

By the end of 1908, Bunty had sold or given away sixty-three paintings in the year. The proceeds of sale amounted to more than three hundred pounds; it was not a fortune but it was sufficient to give him some independence; this, together with the success of his first exhibition, clearly encouraged him. He took his first studio in Edinburgh the following year.

His new found confidence reflected itself in his work and the paintings that emerged in the following year and beyond, were quite different in subject matter, tone and style from those that he had previously produced. Cadell, the Colourist, was about to arrive.

Plate 11

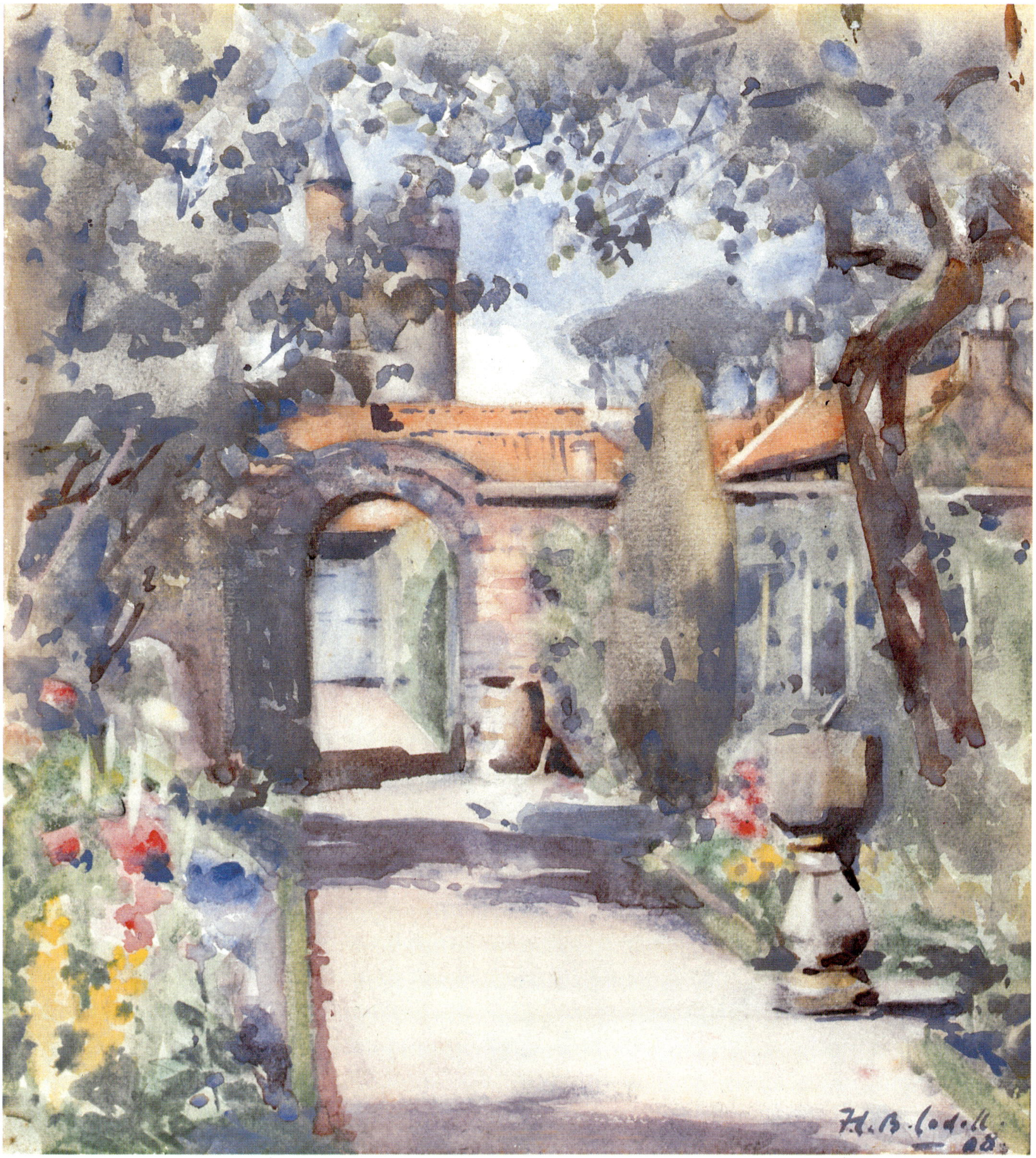

Garden at Grange, 1908 watercolour 11 × 9 in.

Plate 12

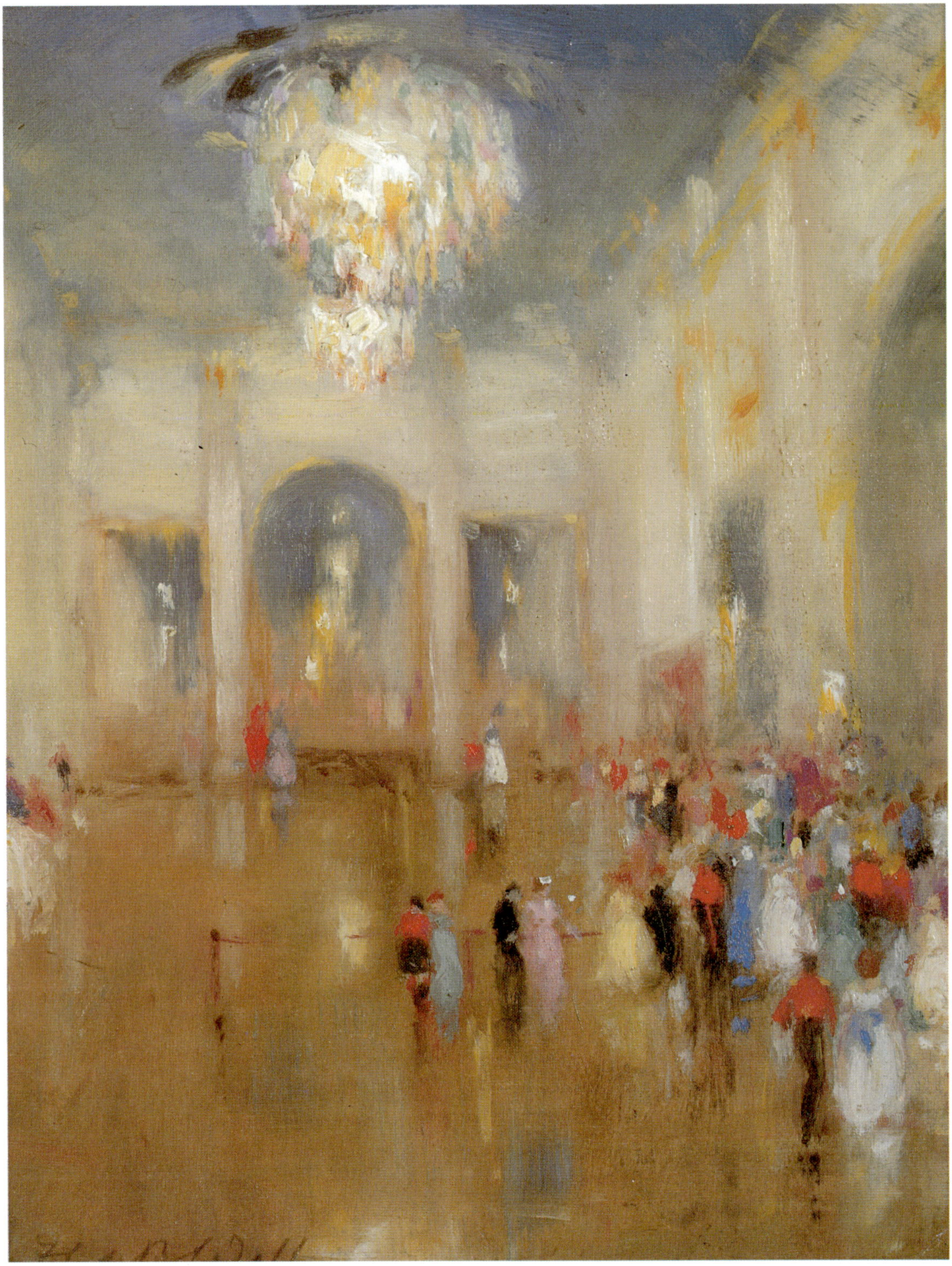

Assembly Rooms, 1908 oil 9 × 7 in.

Chapter Two

1909–1913

Early in 1909, Bunty's father died. He had been unwell for over two years and, although his death was not wholly unexpected, it was a distressing blow for the family; not unnaturally, it brought Bunty and Jean even closer together (their younger brother, Arthur, was serving in the army in India at the time).

A small inheritance was left to Bunty and this was used to secure his first studio at 137 George Street. It was one of six studios that he had in Edinburgh at different stages of his career. Inevitably, it took time to commission the studio and to wind up his late father's estate so, before moving into 137 George Street, Bunty made several trips to stay with friends. One such trip was to the Fords' house, Wester Dunes, at North Berwick. He returned regularly to North Berwick, enjoying not only the Fords' friendship and hospitality but also the company of other artists who either lived in or visited the town. Patrick Adam, the well known painter of interiors, had a house nearby, and Peploe was a regular visitor.

Before leaving Wester Dunes, Bunty presented the Fords with a formal portrait of Mrs Ford, together with a less formal oil sketch entitled, *'Mrs Ford in the Garden'*. The latter, (Plate 13), helps to highlight the new direction of his work and the development of a softer, more impressionist palette.

Back in Edinburgh, and at last moved into his first studio, Bunty received a commission to paint the portrait of Mrs Pelham Burn, dressed in a black evening dress; it was probably the catalyst which alerted him to a theme (the lady in black) to which he returned on many occasions throughout his career.

By the autumn of 1909, the disruption caused by his father's death and moving house had given way to the excitement and apprehension of his one man show at Aitken Dott, the gallery run by Mr P. MacOmish Dott and George Proudfoot. Many young Scottish artists of the day felt fortunate to have dealers such as Aitken Dott in Edinburgh and Alexander Reid in Glasgow to promote their works, but Bunty himself often preferred to show his work privately or at the Society of Eight, where he felt that he had more control and was not liable to pay twenty-five or thirty per cent commission.

The exhibition at Aitken Dott was a limited success, with only five paintings finding buyers – two to Patrick Ford. One of these was the glorious still life *'White Peonies'* (Plate 14) which underlined the beautifully rich style that was to be the hallmark of most of the work which he produced before the end of the war. The other paintings that sold were similar in style – three still lifes and an interior of a lady in white on a chintz sofa. It was clear, however, that most members of the Edinburgh art-buying public were still a little uncomfortable with Bunty's rather too modern style with which they were not familiar. Bunty was undeterred, and agreed to hold another show at Aitken Dott in the autumn of the following year. It was at this exhibition that the public was first able to see the brilliant fruits of the several months that he spent in Venice during 1910.

The trip to Venice would not have been possible without some outside financial support. Bunty asked Patrick Ford to sponsor the venture. The basis of their agreement was noted by Bunty in his records, as follows:

"Cheque from P. J. Ford Esq.: £150 to go to Venice and paint. He to choose equivalent in pictures on my return".

Plate 13

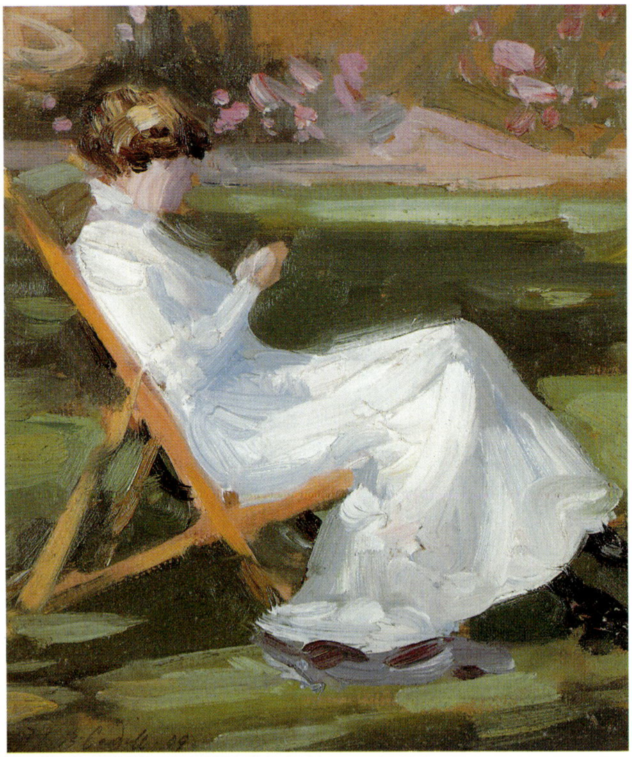

Mrs Ford in the Garden, 1909 oil 10 × 8 in.

Plate 14

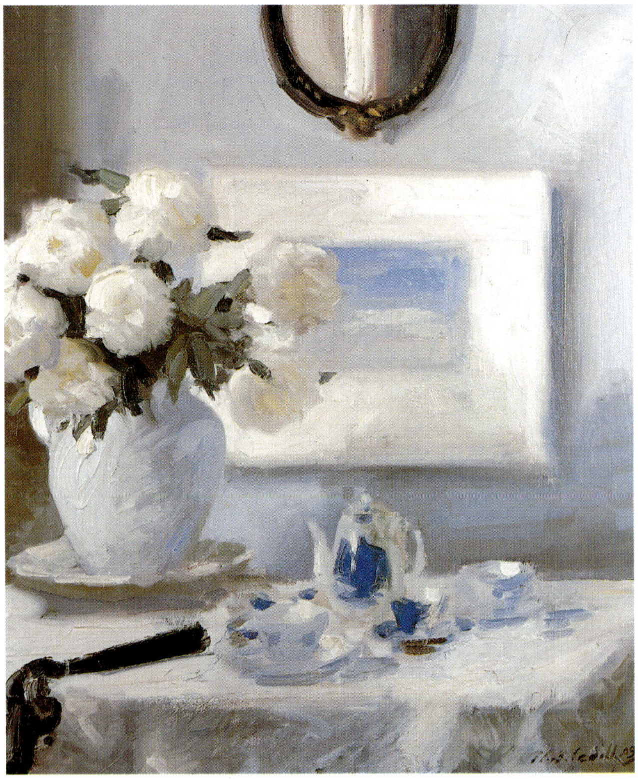

White Peonies, 1909 oil 30 × 25 in.

The effect of Venice on Bunty and his work was dramatic. The combination of the vivid Mediterranean colours with the brilliant sunshine during the day, and the soft warm tones of evening, provided the ideal inspiration for his natural colourist talent. He worked in watercolour and in oil – on large canvasses and small panels, trying to capture not only the wide range of tone and colour, but also the atmosphere of the city. His studies of the 'traditional' canal scenes and church interiors were masterly; but some truly exceptional work was produced when portraying the informal elegance of the city's social life. The series of panels of Florian's café in St. Mark's Square (eg Plate 2) vividly illustrate his uninhibited joy at being part of the vibrant and colourful Venetian atmosphere.

On his return to Edinburgh in the autumn, Bunty duly finalised the details of the Aitken Dott exhibition to be held between 16th and 20th November. However, as sponsor of the trip, Patrick Ford was entitled to make his selection of the Venice paintings ahead of anyone else. The £150 advance that he had given Bunty was converted into six paintings – one exterior view and two interiors of the Salute, a view of St. Mark's Square, one of San Giorgio Maggiore, and the last, the landing stage outside the hotel where he stayed. In addition, the Fords purchased another four paintings before the Aitken Dott directors were able to select the material for their exhibition.

As in the previous year, the exhibition itself was only moderately successful. Six paintings were sold – three oils and three watercolours. It was perhaps this which helped to convince Bunty that he could do just as well by organising his own exhibitions and that there was

Plate 15

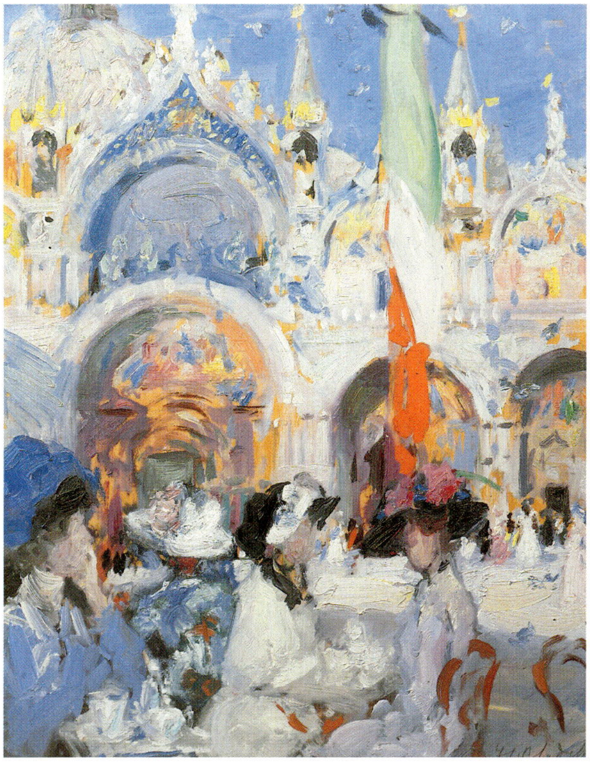

Florian's Café, Venice, 1910 oil 18 × 15 in.

Plate 16

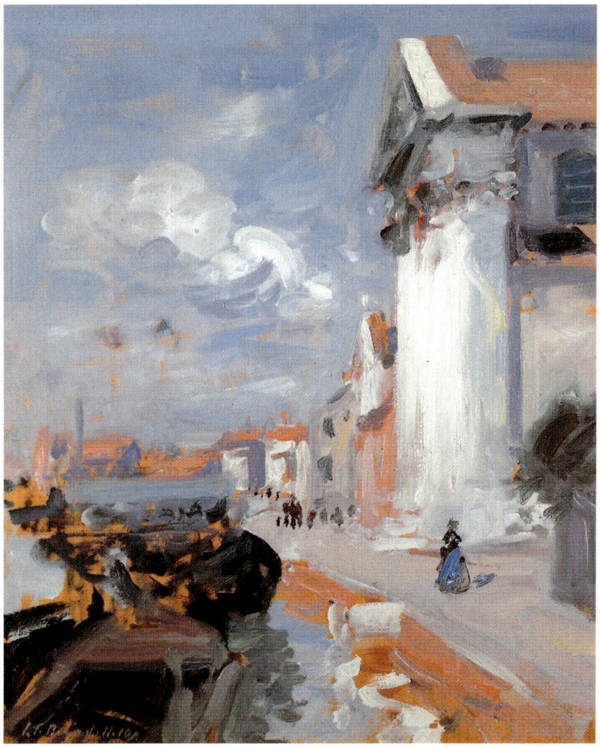

Santa Maria della Salute, 1910 oil 18 × 15 in.

Plate 17

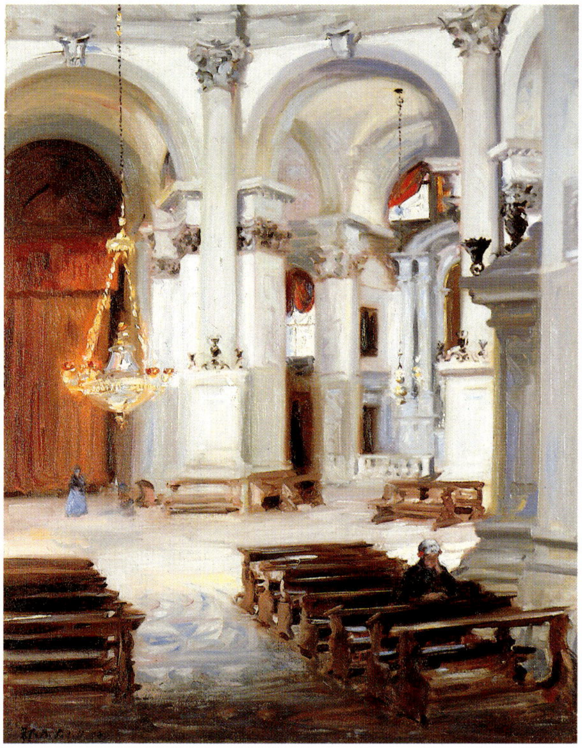

Interior Salute, Venice, 1910 oil 46 × 36 in.

Plate 18

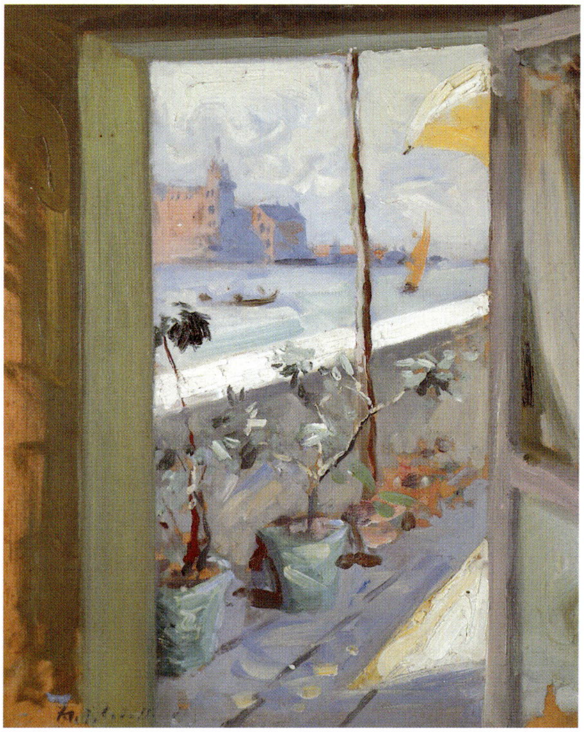

From the Balcony, 1910 oil 18 × 15 in.

Plate 19

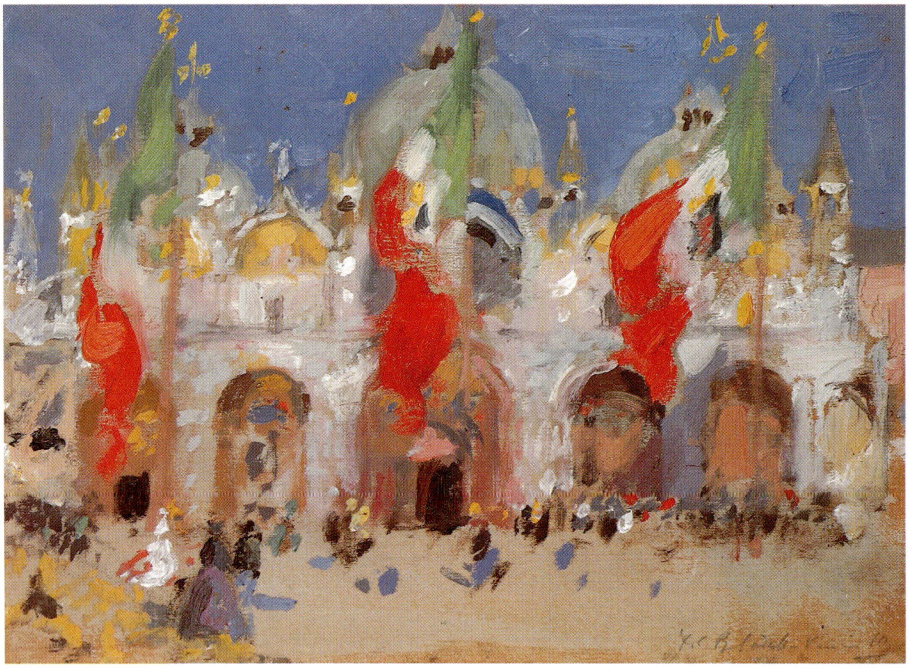

St Mark's Square, Venice, 1910 oil 8 × 12 in.

probably no better salesman of his own paintings than himself. Certainly, there is no record of another exhibition with any other dealer until 1917, when he showed with Doig, Wilson and Wheatley in Edinburgh and with both Alexander Reid and George Davidson in Glasgow.

Also, Bunty thrived on company and welcomed and encouraged friends and potential customers to visit him. Those who did so regularly called after mid-day, in the knowledge that an active social life and a natural inclination towards sleeping late, meant that Bunty was not always at his best in the early morning.

Bunty gave half a dozen of his Venetian paintings to friends and family. Jean, his sister, who was by now married and called Perceval-Clark, received a beautiful view of St. Mark's Square (Plate 19), while James Paterson, his fellow artist and co-founder of the Society of Eight, was given an enchanting watercolour of the Old Palace.

By the end of 1910, Bunty had to revert to producing at least some works in the more accepted traditional style to afford the luxuries of life that he desired. For, from an early age it had been clear that he had a flamboyant and stylish sense of dress, and an appetite for both good food and wine. Not that he was a sybarite, rather that his optimistic and outgoing personality meant that he liked to live life to its fullest and encouraged others to do likewise. He was a generous host who loved nothing better than entertaining friends with an equally quick wit and happy disposition. Unfortunately, while this did much to bolster his reputation as a host, it did nothing to improve his bank balance. He was never a wealthy man, relying purely on the sale of his paintings to support his lifestyle. In only eight years of his life did his income exceed one thousand pounds, and in many years, particularly towards the

Plate 20

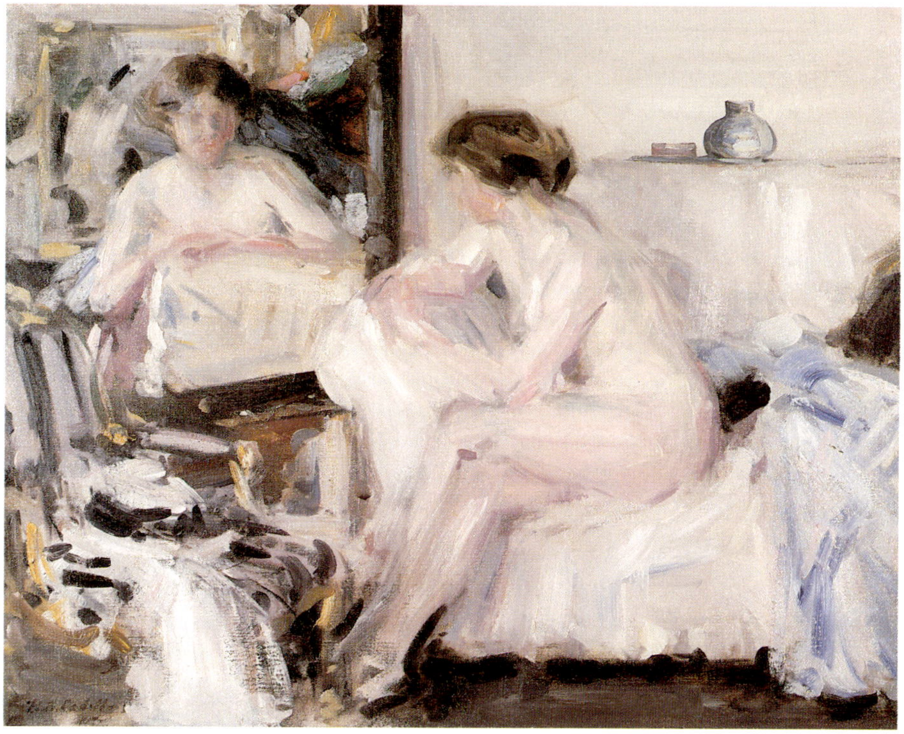

Nude – Reflections, c, 1912 oil 20 × 30 in.

Plate 21

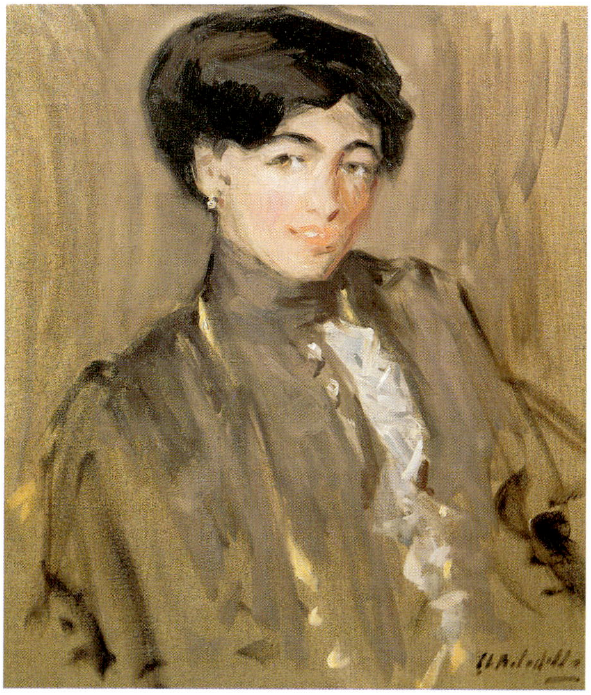

Mrs Chiene, 1912 oil 24 × 20 in.

Plate 22

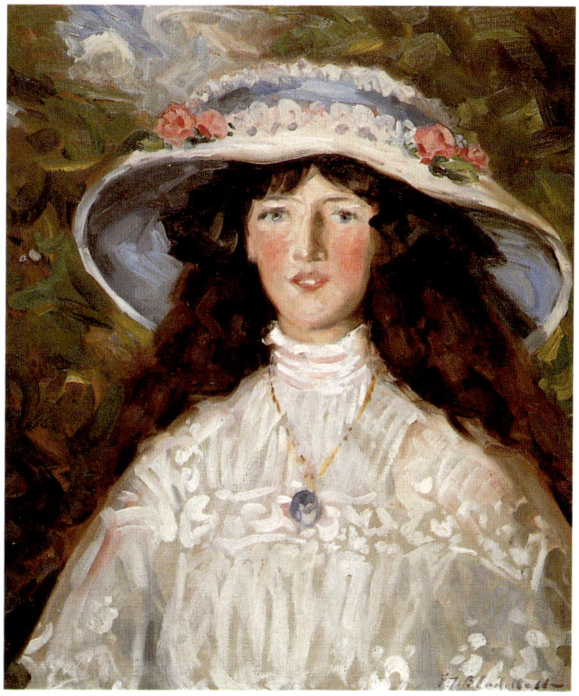

Valentine Ford, 1911 oil 30 × 25 in.

end of his life, it was less than five hundred. To Bunty, however, this was relatively unimportant; what mattered was his belief that life was to be enjoyed and that he was able to impart his enjoyment to others.

His more inspired works of 1911 clearly demonstrate this. For, while Bunty produced nine portraits, among which was that of *'Valentine Ford'* (Plate 22), together with a dozen traditional landscapes in oil and watercolour, he also sold his first studio interior. The painting was exhibited at the Royal Glasgow Institute of Fine Art (R.G.I.), and won the Art Union Prize. Another interior followed, this time of Patrick Ford's dining room at Wester Dunes, probably inspired by Patrick Adam. But, perhaps some of the finest works of 1911 and later were the sumptuous interiors often featuring one of his favourite models, the noted beauty, Miss Don Wauchope. She sat for Bunty on numerous occasions, as the model for the series of oils that he produced over the next fifteen years on the theme of *'Lady in a Black Hat'*. She obviously shared Bunty's taste for fine clothes; her brilliantly coloured robe was the focal point of the painting illustrated in Plate 29.

By the end of 1911, arrangements were well in hand for the formation of the Society of Eight which was officially founded the following year. It was Bunty's concept that a society of like minded artists, with fixed limited membership and permanent premises could produce an annual exhibition of a uniformly higher standard than the 'general' exhibitions which took place at the Royal Scottish Academy and the Royal Glasgow Institute. Comprised of three members of the Glasgow School and five Edinburgh artists, the Society cut across the traditional Edinburgh/Glasgow artistic divide. Bunty's fellow founding members were Patrick Adam, David Alison, James Cadenhead, John Lavery, Harrington Mann, James Paterson and A. G. Sinclair. Premises were taken at 12 Shandwick Place in Edinburgh and the suite of rooms used for the annual exhibition was named 'The New Gallery'. The annual subscription was seven pounds five shillings.

An exhibition was held every year, at which each artist was entitled to show about twenty works. The prestigious 'front wall' of the gallery was used by the members in rotation, while the secretary's annual fee took the form of a painting of his choice from that artist's exhibits. Occasionally, guests were invited to submit work, and Peploe often did so before he, himself, was elected a member. Bunty went to great efforts to ensure that his best work was available for the Society of Eight exhibition and if work of sufficient quality was not available, he would often borrow paintings back from those to whom he had sold them.

The Society's first exhibition opened on 14th November 1912. One of those to purchase a drawing by Bunty was Ivor Campbell, grandson of the eighth Duke of Argyll, and a distant Cadell relative. Bunty was subsequently invited to stay with the Campbells and it was during a visit to Inverary Castle that the Duke of Argyll gave him the splendid kilt of Campbell tartan which he regularly wore with such natural panache.

The formation of the Society of Eight and the support of its members, obviously helped to give Bunty the confidence to paint more extensively in his natural free flowing and spontaneous style; as a result, 1912 was notable for a succession of still life paintings, interiors and portraits of a delightfully uninhibited nature. The informal oil sketch of *'Lady in White'*, (Plate 23), was followed by a series of ten drawings entitled, *'Wrestlers'* (Plate 95) which were donated to the New Unionist Club in Edinburgh. His portraits took on a more relaxed and elegant character as evidenced by the painting of Mrs Chiene (Plate 21), the wife of George Chiene, another of Bunty's loyal friends and patrons.

With two new works, (*'Lady in Black'* and *'The Mirror'*), accepted by the R.S.A., it was a rather more cheerful and optimistic young man that set out in the late summer for a visit to the island of Iona, just off the west coast of Mull. It was a trip that had a profound influence

Plate 23

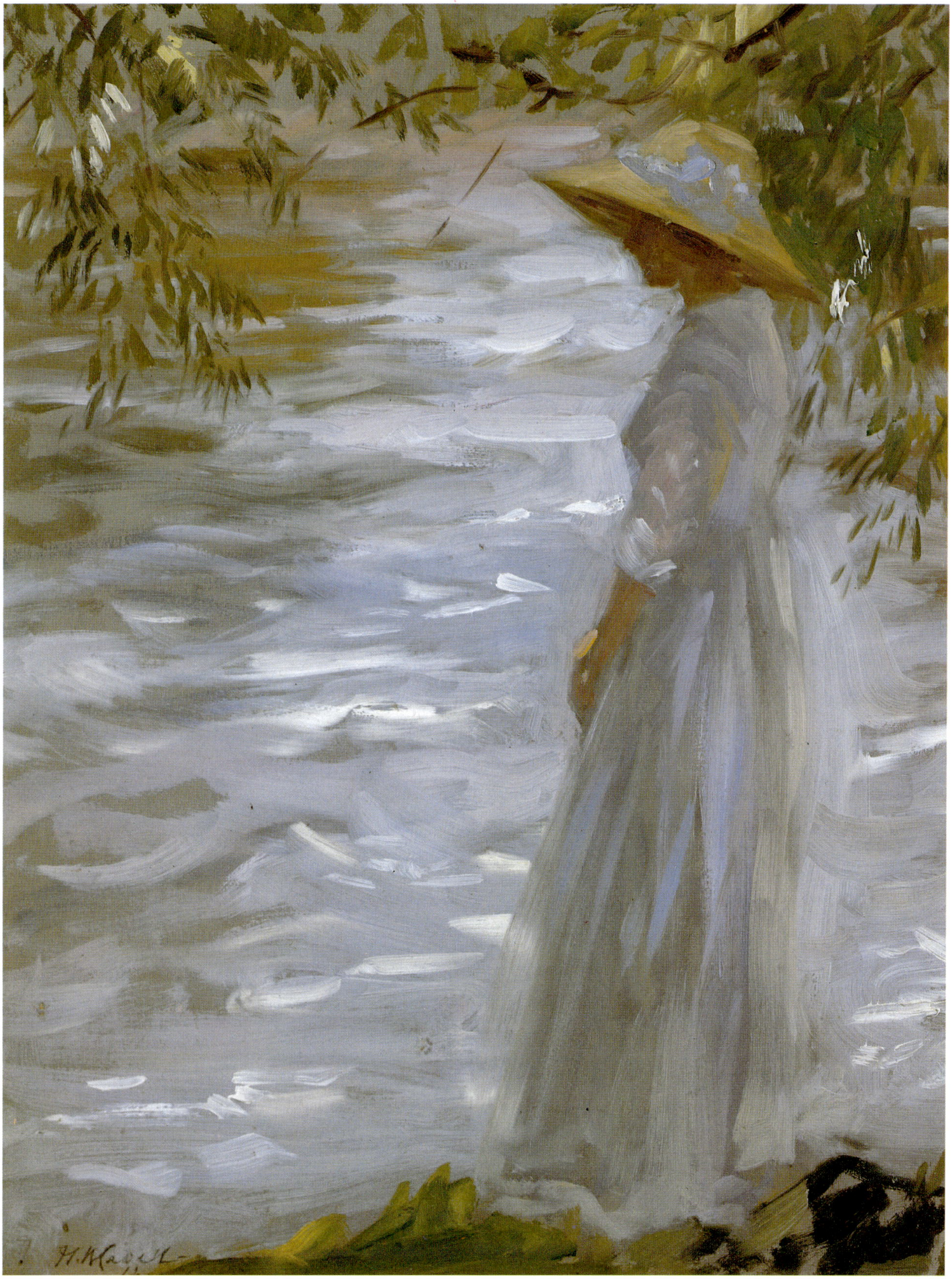

Lady in White, 1912 oil 18 × 15 in.

Plate 24

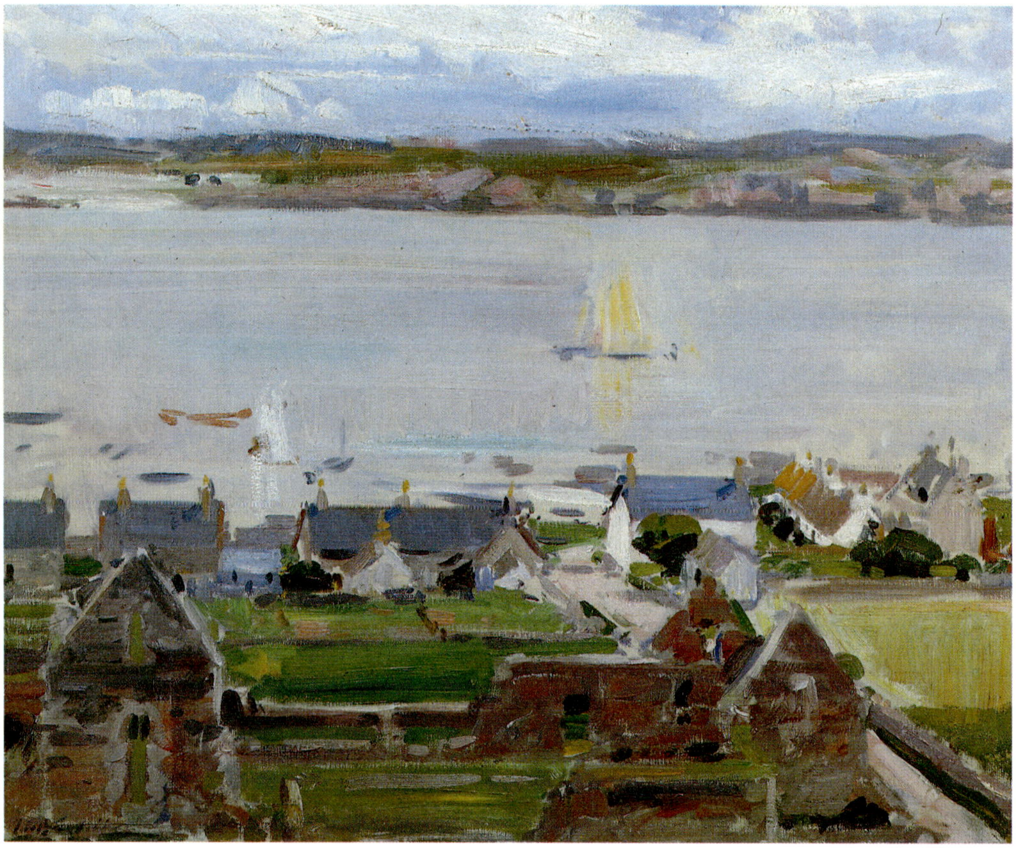

The Nunnery, Iona, c. 1913 oil 25 × 30 in.

on Bunty who fell in love with the place and returned almost every year for the rest of his life. He was fascinated by the brilliant sparkling colours of the water, and by the contrasting tones of rocks and shoreline; by the almost mesmeric perspective of distant islands, and above all by the rapidly changing light. It was his uncanny ability to instantly capture that particular light and precise colour, however fleeting, that ensured that the island was a constant source of inspiration and fulfilment for him.

Bunty's engaging personality meant that he soon established friendships with the local inhabitants and 'elders' in the island community. He stayed at the St. Columba Hotel, and, until renting his own cottage, used a small room at the back of the hotel as a studio. He also quickly became a familiar and welcome face among the many mainland families who took their summer holidays on the island. Indeed, it was during his first visit to Iona that he met George Service who was to become one of his greatest patrons, decorating almost every room in his houses in Glasgow and Dumbartonshire with Bunty's paintings.

By the end of 1912, Bunty had decided to change studio in Edinburgh and, early in 1913, moved into 130 George Street. Eager to return to the west coast, he set out for Iona on July 15th for a ten week summer stay. It was more than a working holiday – it was a chance to reflect and to enjoy the freedom and challenges that the island offered. One Sunday, sitting on a hill above the church, he started to write a poem which he never finished; its title was 'One Sunday at Iona'.

Plate 25

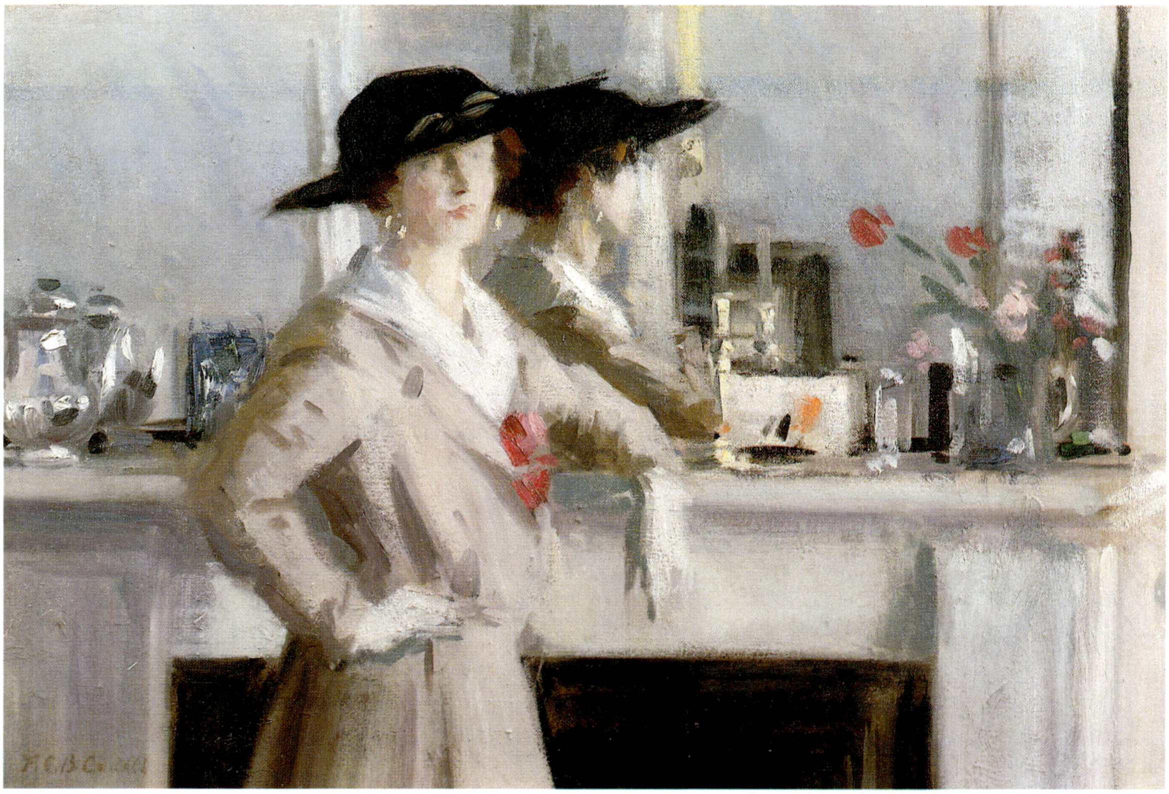

Reflections (Summer), c. 1913 oil 22 × 32 in.

"Warmed by the sun, blown by the wind I sat
Upon the hill top looking at the Sound.
Down in the church beneath, the people sat
On chairs and laughed and frowned.

No chairs for me when I can lie
And air myself upon the heather
And watch the fat bees buzzing by
And smell the smell of summer weather.

Let them bow down to God unfound
For me the sound that stretches round
For me the flowery scented ground
Upon the hilltop looking at the sound.

No church for me to worship in
Confined by walls of dank dark stone.
For rather can I worship him
When I am out in his fair world."

This poem helps to illustrate Bunty's deep affection for the island. His paintings found ready buyers both in the local community and in those on holiday. By the time he returned

Plate 26

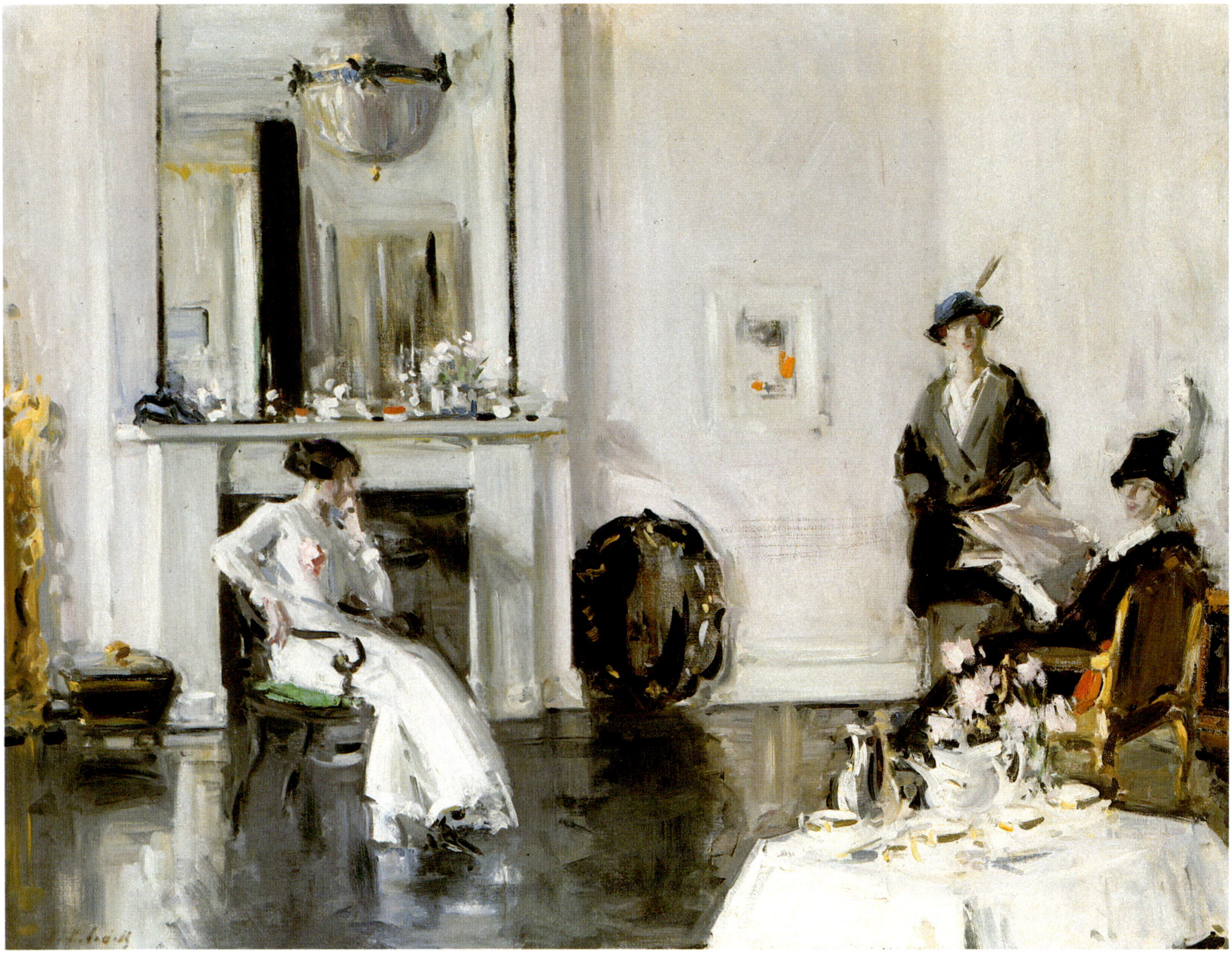

Afternoon, 1913 oil 40 × 50 in.

to Edinburgh at the end of September, he had sold eighteen paintings of the island for over £300, including five to the Service family.

Late in the year he put the finishing touches to his largest interior painting to date (Plate 26). He gave it the simple title '*Afternoon*'; it was not shown until 1915, when it was exhibited at the R.S.A. and purchased for £80 by W. H. Raeburn Esq., of West Nile Street, Glasgow. Without doubt, it was one of his most luscious works of the period – and of a style that never really re-emerged in his work after the end of the war. To a certain extent, it was a swansong of the innocent and idealistic Edwardian era.

Chapter Three

1914–1919

Bunty spent much of the spring and summer of 1914 on Iona. While he was there he received a letter from the secretary of the Venice International Exhibition about two works which he had entered for sale.

"I have the great pleasure to announce you an offer for your two works *'Ballet Girl'* – 100 francs and *'Cecilia'* – 100 francs, for the sum of 180 francs. Your two works will be offered from the purchaser to our Gallery of Modern Art in Venice and will be exhibited there in the especial collection of Black and White".

Bunty sold the drawings, receiving £4 for each. He also sold three more drawings to Ivor Campbell, and finished G. W. Service's commission to paint his three children, before returning to Edinburgh to volunteer for the army, following Britain's declaration of war on August 4th. In the meantime he had received word from Ted Stewart supporting Pat Adam's suggestion that the Society of Eight Exhibition should not be held that year because of the outbreak of war. Seven of the members agreed; Bunty did not. On September 2nd he wrote from Iona.

"I am entirely at variance with Pat Adam's proposal. I think it would be both unpatriotic and unbusiness like in the extreme were we not to hold our annual exhibition as usual. All the world knows that the Government of this country has made every effort to maintain a normal situation and their success in this laudable ambition largely depends on the assistance they receive from individual societies.

Not to have an exhibition would show that we were afraid of financial failure at the cost of giving the picture loving of the public a little much needed relaxation.

Why in God's name should we not have a show – are we a beaten nation? The complete cessation of commercial enterprise which our otherwise excellent Chairman advocates, savours too strongly of a downtrodden and depressed people. In my opinion it is our duty to our country to hold a show and lose by it if necessary, provided we, by doing so, help to preserve the national equilibrium.

No, Mr Adam's proposal sniffs too strongly of the death chambers of the vanquished . . . We ought to have our 'War Number', only one let us hope, and by so doing show ourselves to be a victorious, joyous, prosperous society rather than a fearful, trembling, tottering collection of old wives waiting to see which way the wind blows.

So, have the show and give the gate money to the War Fund."

Bunty's will prevailed, and the third exhibition of the Society of Eight was held in November 1914.

To his surprise and obvious disappointment, Bunty's application to join the army was turned down. The culprit was his beloved pipe, the medical examination revealing that he suffered from 'smoker's heart'. Determined to fulfil his responsibilities, Bunty spent the next months working on a farm near Dumfries in a successful attempt to improve his fitness sufficiently to pass the medical board's second examination late the following year. He joined the Royal Scot's Guards as an ordinary soldier and was appropriately posted to the 'Dandy Ninth' regiment where, in a typically flamboyant gesture, he arranged to have his standard issue uniform replaced with one of fine quality cloth made for him by his Edinburgh tailor.

It was not until late 1915, that Bunty was posted to serve on the French front. Before leaving he produced a series of drawings of army life; they were the inspiration for the *'Jack and Tommy'* book, which was published in 1916 by Grant Richards in London. Sixteen of the drawings were sold at the Society of Eight Exhibition in November for a total of one hundred pounds. Of this, ten pounds went in commission to the Society, while Bunty donated a further forty pounds to the Scottish branch of the Red Cross. This generosity was typical; he gave away further works to various charities that supported victims of the war, without any consideration of his own financial position which was by no means secure.

In Edinburgh, Bunty continued to live life to the full, particularly in the company of other artists. Peploe had already become a close friend who, although of a less outgoing character than Bunty, was not averse to occasionally participating in the 'artistic evenings' that were often arranged at 130 George Street. Another close companion of the time was the extrovert sculptor, Pittendrigh Macgillivray, who wrote to Bunty shortly after finishing his 'La Flandre' bust.

"Herewith a copy of a sonnet evoked by the La Flandre bust, which may interest you. I wonder if I might find you in your den about eight on Monday evening when we might talk of floods of colour and many other wonderful paintly things?"

After their meeting, Macgillivray again wrote to Bunty.

"I have been thinking of your work and our talk about it, last evening. It seems to me more than ever clear that your forté lies in a gift of colour and light – these seen in a joyous mood. The little scrap sketches with which you are now playing, seem to me morbid and off line; . . . I imagine I am right in believing you have something far better and happier to express – far more of sun and colour, and joy of spiritual health to give out . . . Take wing! Be glad you live! and help others to have your gift of happiness . . . Please see that you have more of those excellent biscuits against the next time I come so that the literary result may not be quite so indigestable!"

Bunty's response was to arrange a 'La Flandre' evening, to which Paterson, Peploe and MacGillivray were invited. The success of the event, which lasted until about five the next morning, can be judged by MacGillivray's subsequent letter and poem.

"Your La Flandre evening and morning were A.1. and up to the mark of many an old Glasgow one. Such hours are a grand cure for the general element of stodge apt to creep over artist folk . . . Your caricature is great fun . . . I enclose my version of the entertainment where you'll find yourself set down as cock o' the walk!"

The evening was typical of ones which Bunty hosted throughout his career, and for which he became famous. They were often attended by his close friend Ted Stewart, at whose wedding Bunty was best man prior to leaving for active service. Ted and his bride, Miss Nan Ivory, received a painting each as a wedding present. One was the still life *'Flowers in a Blue Jug'* (Plate 28).

Later that year, his 1913 interior entitled *'Afternoon'* sold at the R.S.A. Exhibition and another *'Interior with Figure'* was sold at the National Society of Portrait Painters Exhibition

La Flandre
1914

On "La Flandre nicht", in MacCadell's trench,
Wi' a keg o' the Dymock's brew,
We sat till four an' we didna flench
In the 'grip o' the mountain dew.

Saint Clair was there wi' his cannie e'e —
The Peploe, keen as a hawk! —
MacCadell himsel' was the cock o' the spree,
But the Pittendrigh he did talk.

Freeaucht we sat — through a lang nicht shift:
Nae heed for the German swine!
For we wur back whar our herts did lift
An' we roastit the "chestnuts" fine!

An' aye we ettle't the ither dram,
Wi' dry oat-cakes for a foond;
An' aye for the "Gluépots" anither "damn!"
Gart the German fleg at the soond!

We hawl't the "Glesga Schule" frae its grave
Whaur it lies in Dunedin's mools;
We linger't their scalps, but — what needs we rave?
"The best — come theday, are but snools!"

Syne the Pittendrigh said — as he liftit at last!
"The keg o' guid Dymock's düne"!
The lave raise up — tho' they lookit seat-fast,
An' we a' thocht — shürely it's süne!

But our watch was bye, an' the lamp gaen oot;
So we snookit to trench to the rear.
But we'll mind that nicht in MacCadell's "dug-oot"
An' the morn that our heids hung sweir!

P.W.

To
Francis C.B. Cadell
as a souvenir o' his "La Flandre nicht"
Thursday March. 4th 1915.

Plate 27

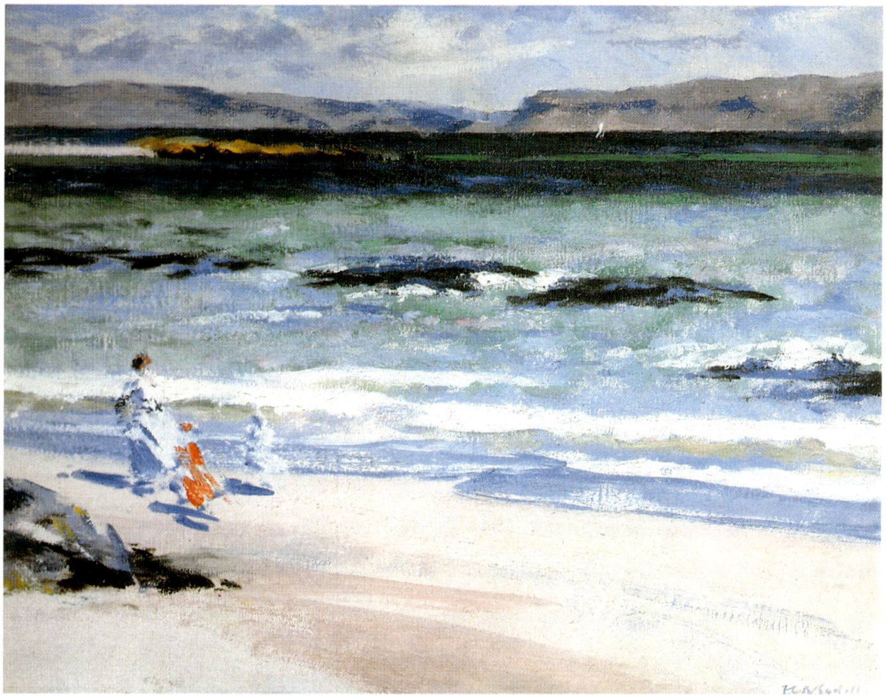

Iona, c. 1914 — oil 15 × 18 in.

Plate 28

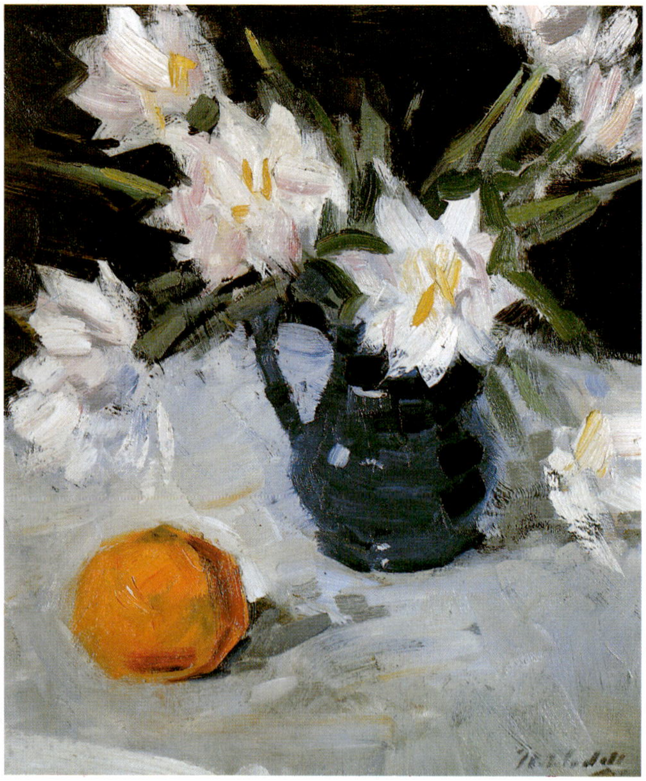

Flowers in a Blue Jug, 1915 oil 18 × 15 in.

Plate 29

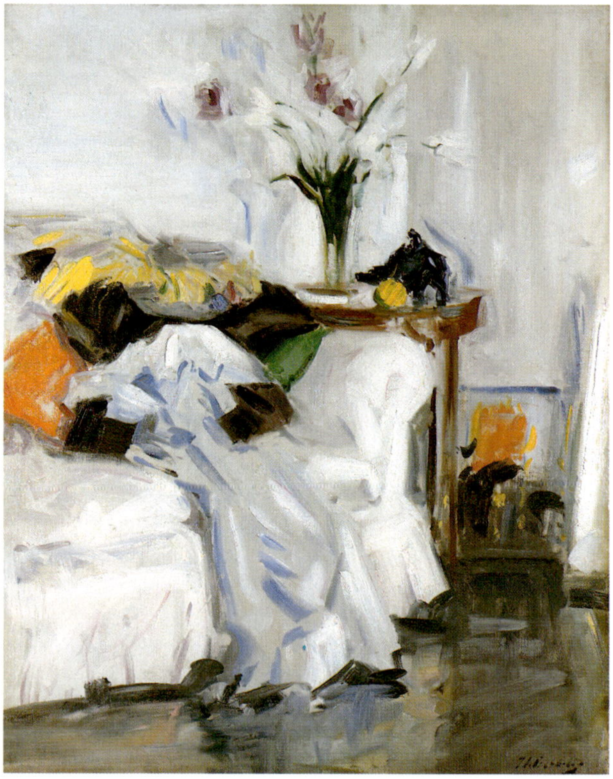

Miss Don Wauchope's Robe, c. 1915 oil 44 × 34 in.

in London. They helped generate some welcome income for Bunty whose output of paintings understandably suffered during his time in the trenches.

For most of 1916 Bunty was in France, occasionally returning home on leave for a few days. Not wanting to miss an opportunity to savour some of the luxuries that were unavailable at the front, he is reputed to have dined regularly at the Savoy wearing his battle stained kilt and to have enjoyed the perplexed looks from officers unused to seeing a private soldier in such surroundings.

While on leave, Bunty arranged for some work, mainly wash drawings, to be shown at the Society of Eight Exhibition. They received good reviews; writing in the Studio, the critic A. Eddington reported:

"These bold sketches, in which with a minimum of line in black, with sometimes a dash of colour introduced, a marvellous completeness of effect is produced, which gives Mr Cadell a place in the front rank of cartoonists".

However, by far and away his most notable 'in absentia' success, was the sale of a large oil '*Portrait of a Lady*', at the Royal Glasgow Institute annual exhibition; it was sold for one hundred pounds, the highest price paid for one of his paintings. It had previously been exhibited in the Society of Eight Exhibition in 1915 when the Studio critic suggested that:

"Mr Cadell is one of the most brilliant of the younger Scottish Colourists much of whose inspiration has come from Parisian study, and, in this example, while preserving all the dash

Plate 30

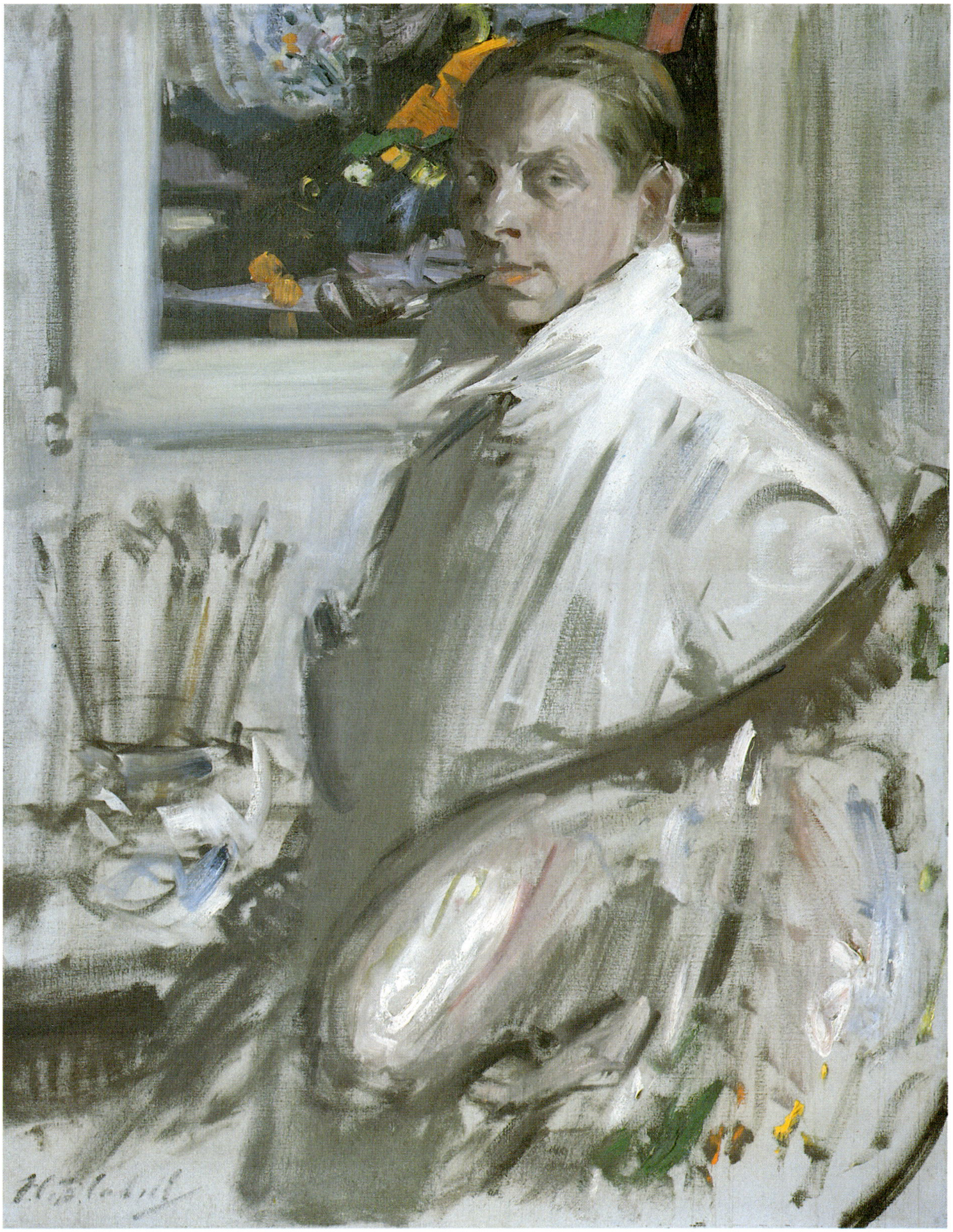

Self-portrait, 1914 oil 50 × 40 in.

Plate 31

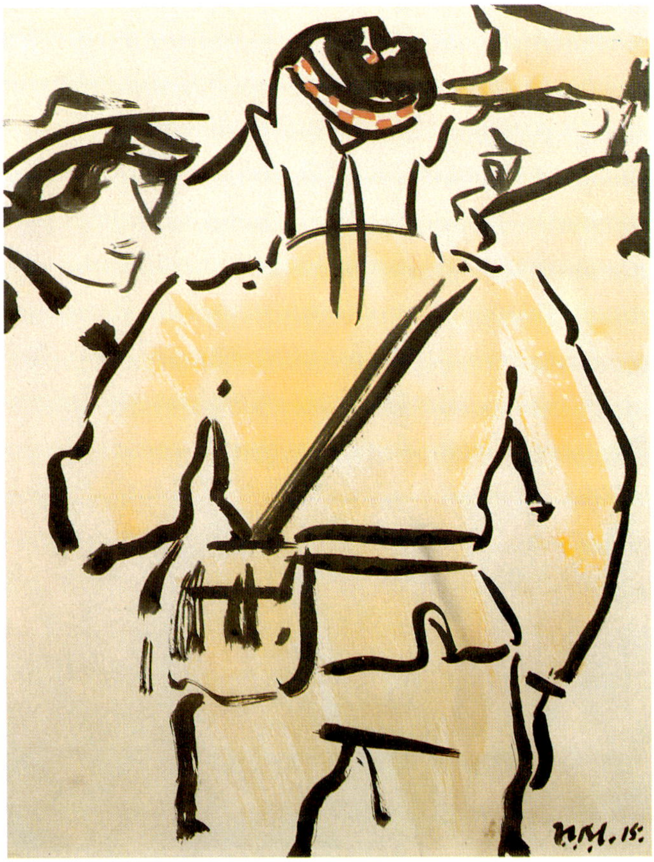

Plate 32

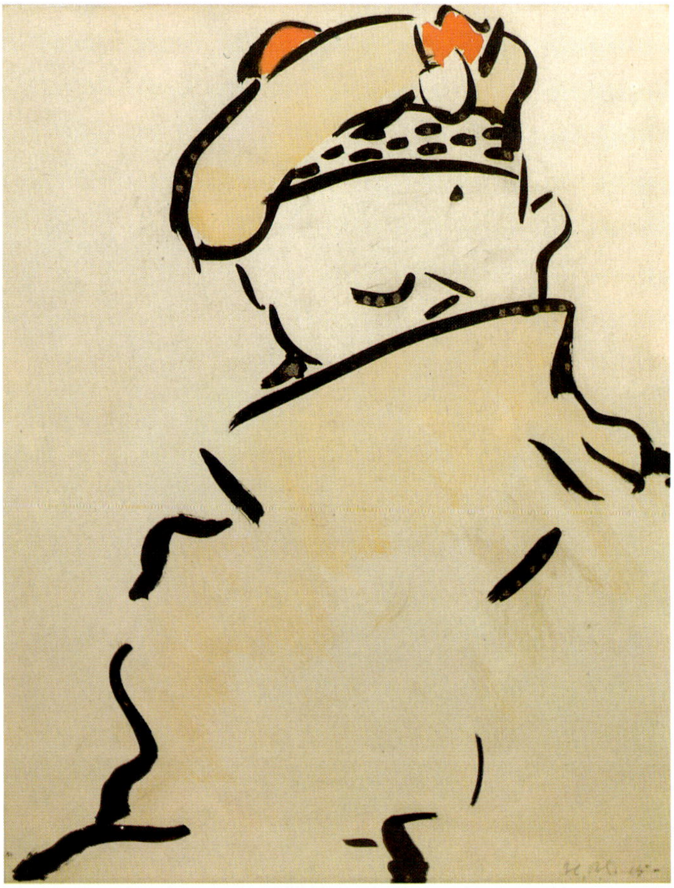

Plate 33

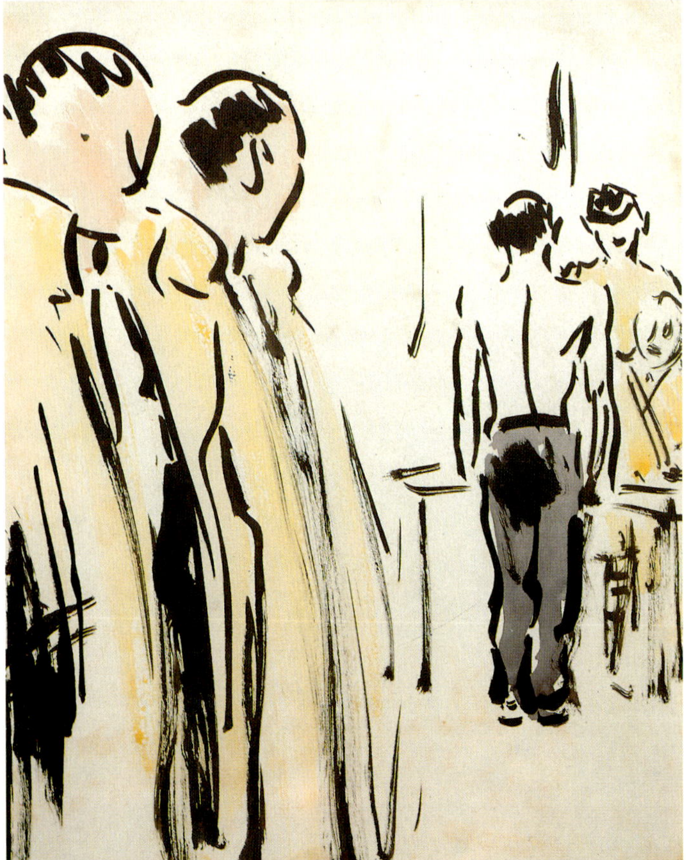

Plate 34

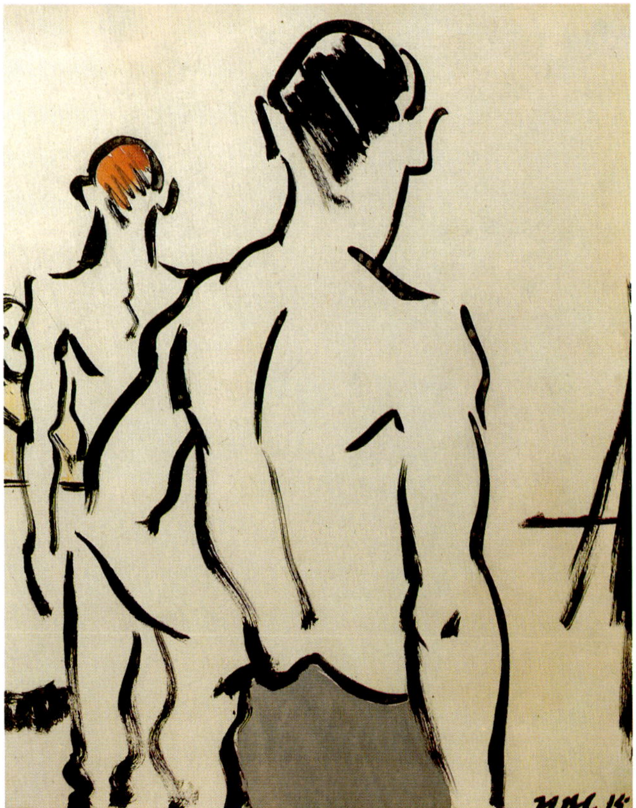

Plate 35

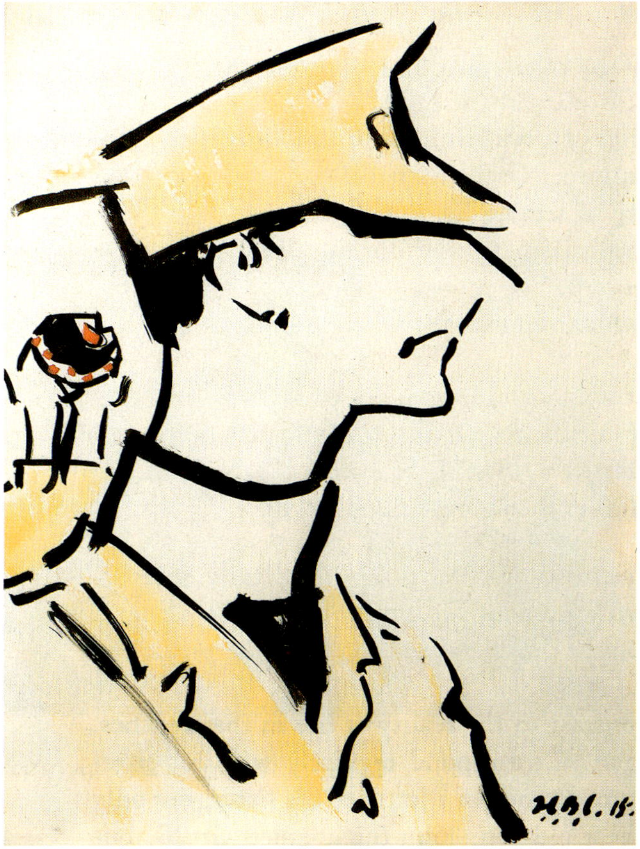

Plate 36

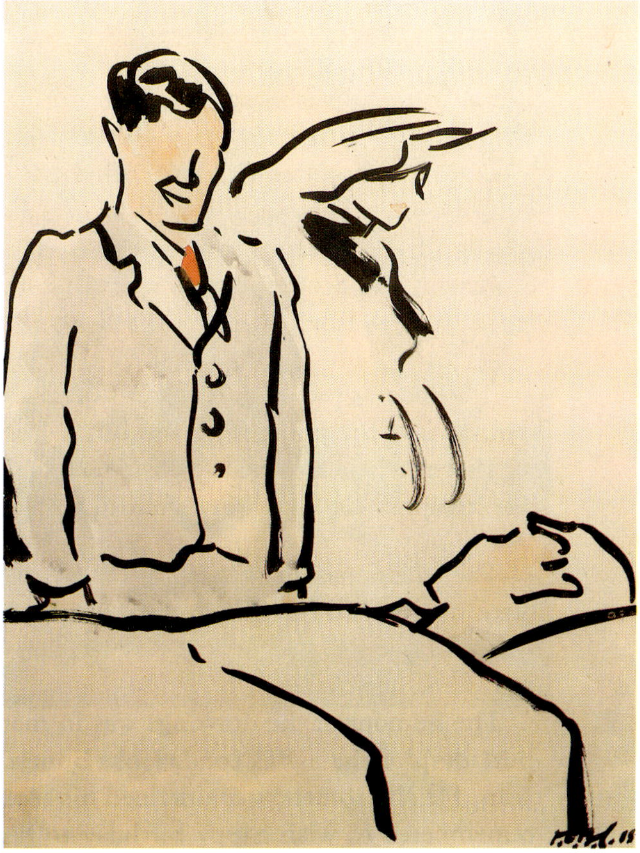

Plate 37

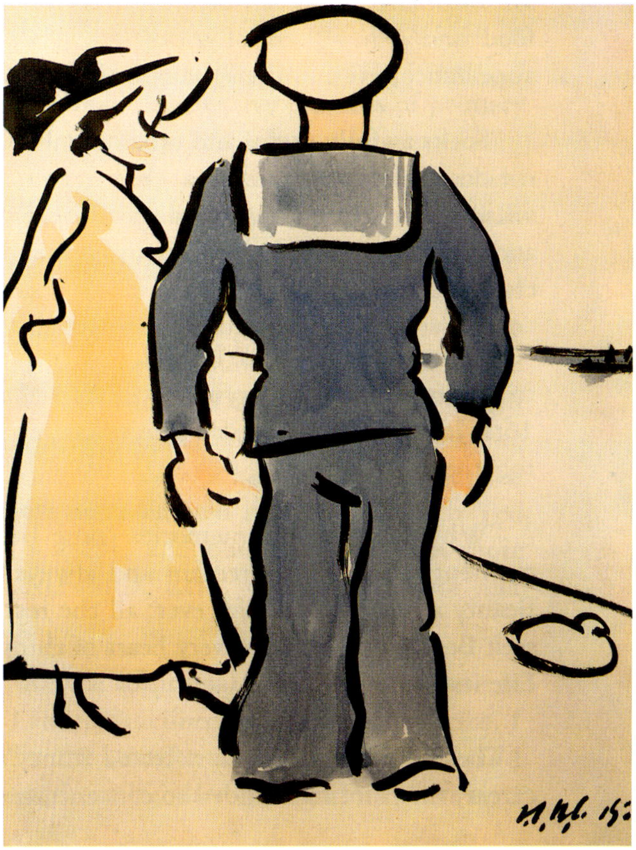

From the 'Jack and Tommy Series', 1915
watercolour and ink $9\frac{1}{2} \times 7$ in.

think I have done pretty well by Cadell and have certainly acquired a number of things which I don't expect to sell within the next ten years. As I explained to you I have done this with the idea of getting the first offer of any more complete decent pictures the artist may have available".

By this time, Bunty had returned briefly from France and was stationed in Ripon undergoing a military training course. He corresponded regularly with Ted Stewart, normally about the price of his paintings that were being sold and with detailed instructions as to which paintings were to be sent to particular dealers and the prices to be asked.

Bunty did, however, find time for leave in London. Ted Stewart was usually called on to settle the various debts that had been incurred. The letter of 20th November is typical of the ones that he received.

CADELL & MORTON, W.S.
LEWIS I. CADELL, W.S.N.P.
W. KINNINBURGH MORTON, B.L., S.S.C.

TELEGRAPHIC ADDRESS, "CADELL, EDINBURGH"
TELEPHONE Nº 2001

REC'D	2 0 NOV 1917
ANS'D	

27 Rutland Square,
Edinburgh 20th November, 1917.

C. E. Stewart, Esq.,
W.S.,
6 Hill Street.

Dear Sir, Mr F. C. B. Cadell.

Mr Cadell called this afternoon and asked us to apply to you for funds to meet various Accounts which have come in. He wishes us to square up with certain London Tailors, and an Account of over £20 has come in from Doig, Wilson & Wheatley which he wishes settled. Various other Accounts have been rendered, and as we recently paid the half years rent of his Studio, we find it will take £107 to clear the balance at his debit in our books and meet these Accounts. We shall accordingly be glad to have your remittance of this amount from the price of some of the pictures he has been selling.

O.
D.

Yours faithfully,
Cadell & Morton

Alexander Reid was now taking an even keener interest in Bunty's work with plans for a one man exhibition during 1918. Reid's support, combined with the proceeds of an exhibition at Doig, Wilson and Wheatley in early December in Edinburgh, meant that Bunty recorded his most successful year to date in terms of income – just under one thousand four hundred pounds. On Ted Stewart's advice, and in typically patriotic fashion, Bunty invested a total of nine hundred pounds in Government War Bonds.

Although successful in financial terms, 1917 had little else to recommend itself from Bunty's personal standpoint. In August he had heard the distressing news of the death of Ivor Campbell. In a touching letter from Dunderave Castle, Lord George Campbell, Ivor's father, wrote:

"Your letter depressed me – why don't you get a commission – surely it would be better. Exactly a year ago I saw Ivor off to France at Dalmally after his leave – it has been a hard four days of memory but better here than in some strange place. I do wish you would get two or

Plate 40

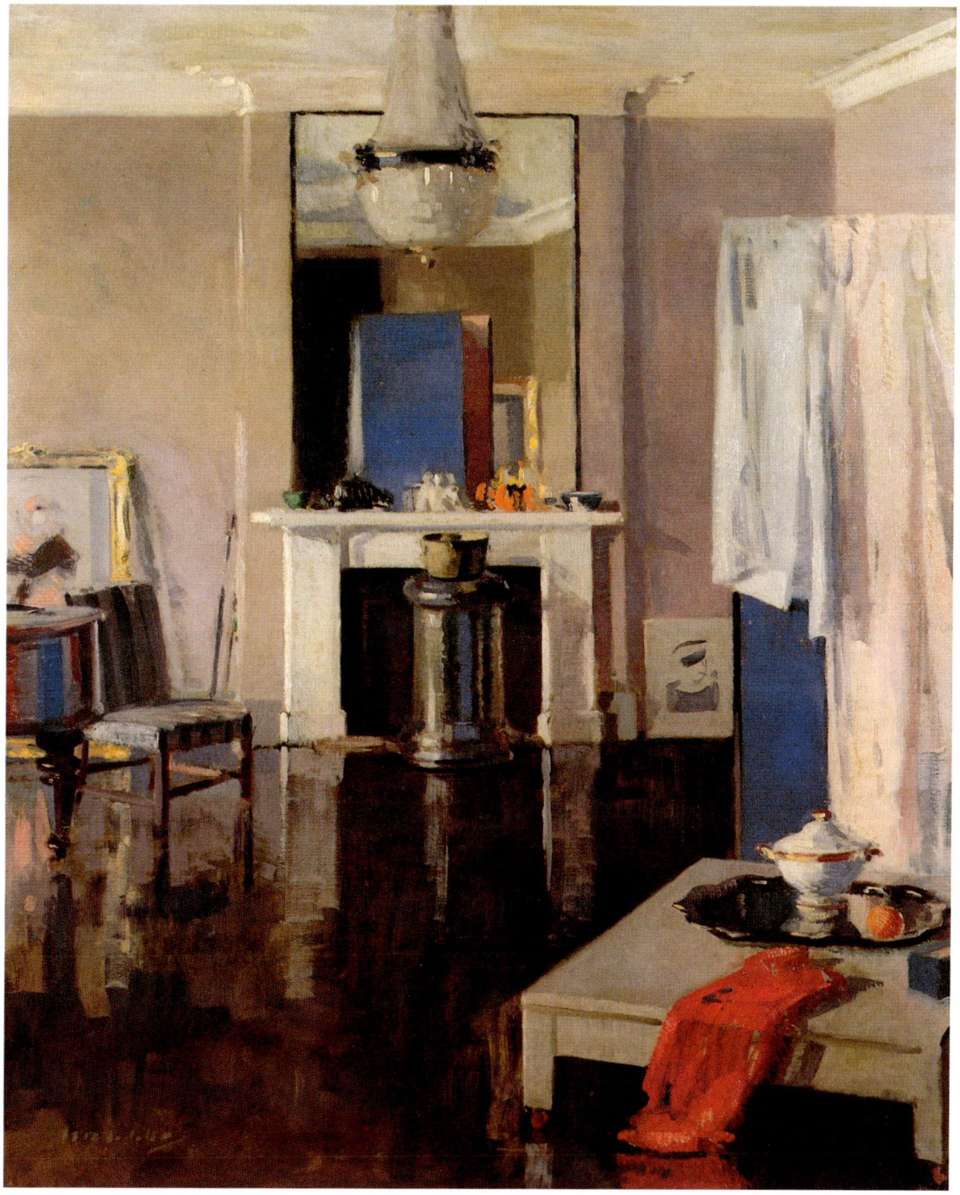

130 George Street, c. 1915 oil 50 × 40 in.

three days leave and come here – though it would be a sad visit for you – every day I want him more and more but the memory of his whole life is very precious. How inconceivably small now his boyish faults seem! and how splendidly he grew up".

Whether it was this exhortation or whether it was at the insistence of his commanding officer, Bunty was finally persuaded to take a commission. Early in 1918 he was appointed a second lieutenant in the 11th Batallion of the Argyll and Sutherland Highlanders. He returned to the front in April before being wounded in July and being sent to recover near Rouen. He kept in regular contact with various friends including Peploe, who wrote to him on June 20th.

Plate 41

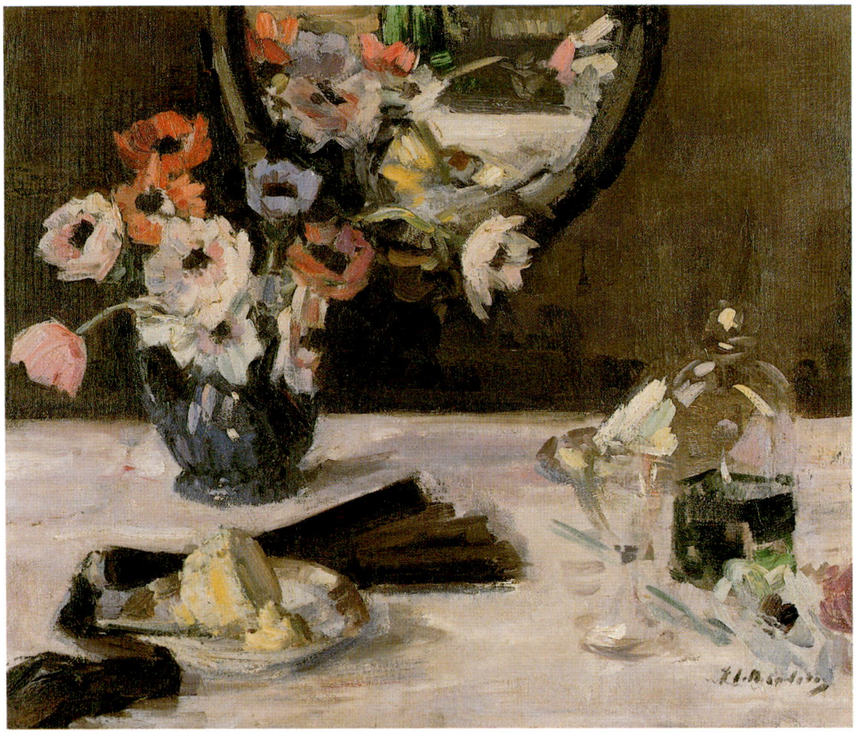

Still Life, c. 1915 oil 18 × 24 in.

"I notice you are using your beautiful sketch book for other uses than you intended, but I can quite understand there can't be much to inspire one in a dug out – I am still in the art business not yet having got my call to serve my King and country! But it won't be long now, I expect. I wish it were over as the present situation is distinctly not good for painting . . . I am finished for good with the colour block system that interested me for a long time and await a new development – what it will be I do not yet quite know – something I think more free and fluent . . . I can see that this habit of yours of living in dugouts must inevitably result in a new development in your painting. I can see you will absolutely give up the use of flake white. After all why shouldn't one. Is it not quite unnecessary for a Colourist? . . . Do you ever see 'colour' in the trenches?"

Peploe wrote again, a month later, having heard that Bunty had been wounded. He, himself, had been turned down once more for military service because of a murmuring heart and was not enjoying his relative loneliness in Edinburgh. He also found it difficult to paint, admitting to Bunty that, on top of everything else:

"The price of paint is getting prohibitive – also scarce. Canvas almost unobtainable. Pictures are also to be taxed twopence in the shilling, so you see life is getting precarious and difficult. There is surely someone in your studio – I see the windows beautifully clean – you haven't given it up, I hope . . . When the war is over I shall go to the Hebrides and recover some virtue I have lost. There is something marvellous about the Western Isles. Of Iona, we must all go there next summer. Wishing you the best of health and a slow recovery!"

Bunty did not recover completely until the closing weeks of the war, and, then only well enough to take up responsibilites away from the front as an officer in charge of German

Plate 42

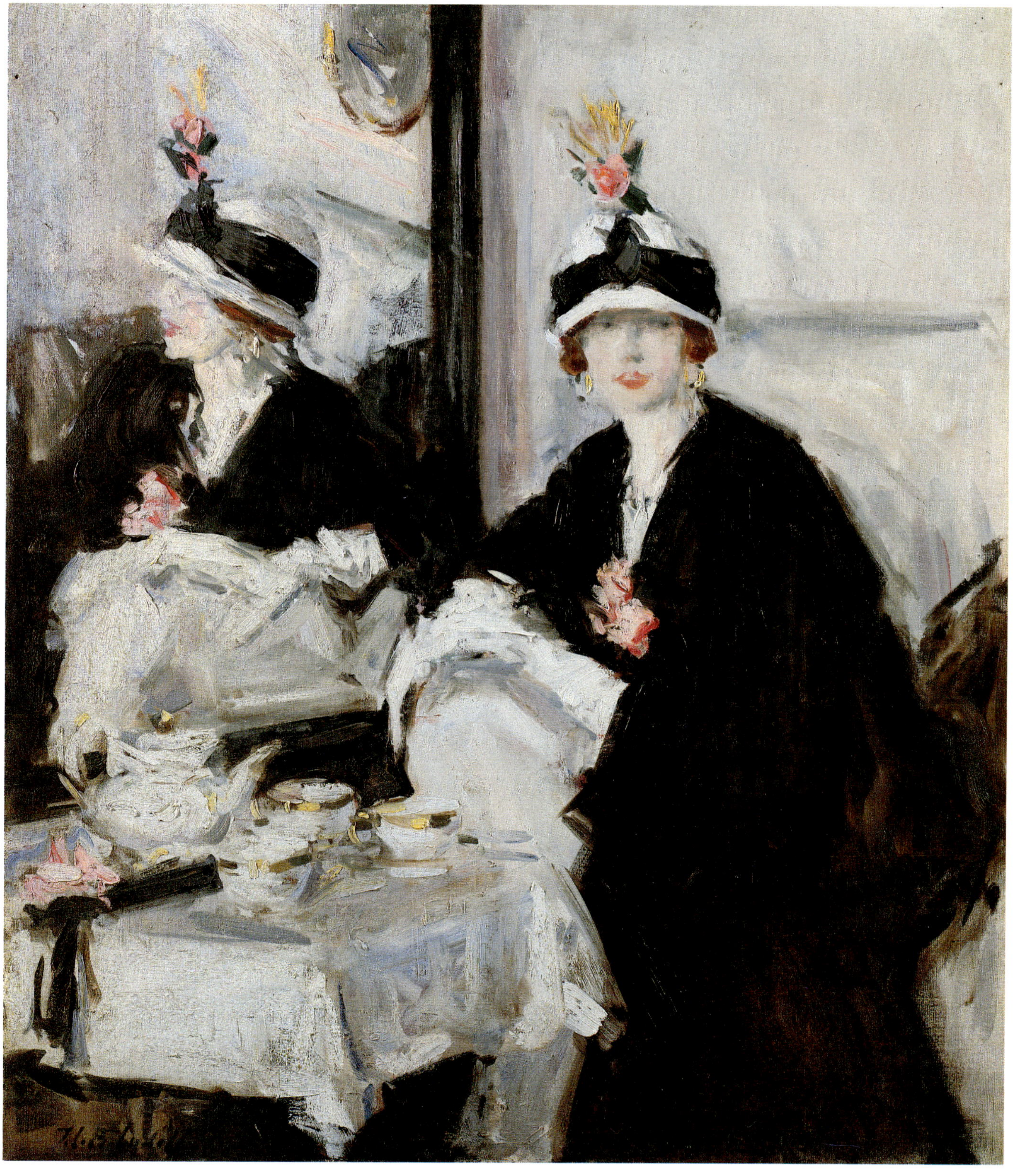

Reflections, c. 1915 oil 46 × 40 in.

Plate 43

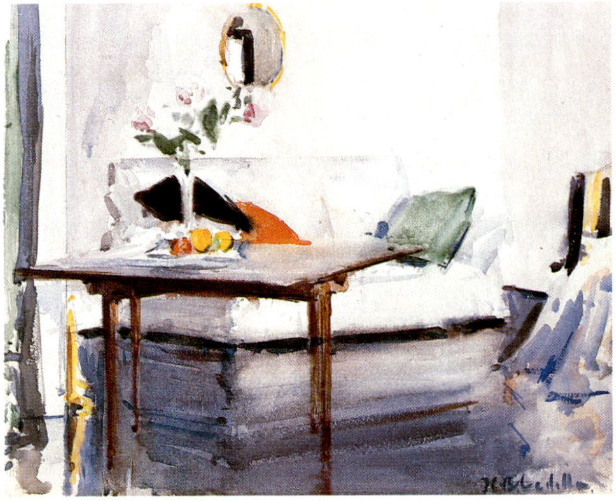

Roses, 1915 watercolour 15 × 18 in.

prisoners of war. In his letters to Jean, he often expressed his deep longing to be back on Iona. On November 6th, when describing an incident at the front in which he had been involved, he wrote:

"But some day, or rather some evening in a future summer, I'll tell you all about it as we sit outside the Columba in deck chairs looking at the Ross of Mull across the Sound of Iona".

His desire to be back on his favourite island was mixed with a deep sense of distress and frustration about what he had experienced during the war. Bunty wrote to Peploe late in 1918, trying to share his pent up anger with his good friend. Peploe replied in early December:

"I think I know how you are feeling. I don't wonder. It must be perfectly hellish. Rather think you will be out of it all and free again. God that will be good. Patience a little longer. I wish I were full of the hate of a thousand years, bottled up concentrated hate – what a magnificent force. I envy you who have this hate, strong motive power. I have used it in my day and know it to be good. Not the best, but good . . . When do you think you will get home? I'm afraid art is not one of the pivotal trades in a modern state, but rather condemned as some foreign substance, like dirt on the rim of the wheel liable at any moment to be dropped off. So be it. It is an idiotic world. It's a long way off, the millenium. Still, in hope, strive, continue. There *is* perfection".

Bunty returned from France in the Spring of 1919. His chief desire was to go as quickly as possible to Iona to rest, to relax, and, above all, to paint. He spent much of the summer on the island, returning to Edinburgh late in the autumn. Until then, he had produced almost no new work in over two years. Although he had benefitted from a highly profitable series of sales in 1917, there was very little of his earlier work left in his studio.

He entered seven still life paintings for the R.S.A. Exhibition and none sold. There was no such problem with the rather timeless Iona landscapes and fifteen were purchased in the four weeks before Christmas directly from Bunty's studio. These sales enabled him to record an income of just under seven hundred pounds for 1919 and to cover the cost of his move to a new studio at 6 Ainslie Place the following year.

Chapter Four

1920–1927

The precise date of Bunty's move to 6 Ainslie Place in 1920 is not known. It is likely that it was in the early autumn, after an extensive stay on Iona that lasted from April until mid September. It is clear, however, that he was still at his studio at 130 George Street in late January when a debate that became known as 'Bolshevism in Colour', began in the columns of the Scotsman. On January 24th, referring to Bunty's work in the Society of Eight annual exhibition which had been brought forward to the beginning of the year, Lady Constance Emmott wrote:

"Is it too much to hope for that our chief art galleries will resolutely leave to rooms in private ownership, the exposure of such flagrant vulgarity and insolent disregard of draughtsmanship as are described to the easily deluded *nouveau riches* as samples of the 'coming art'?

The most hopeless of pessimists will never believe in any widespread acceptance as 'art' of these screaming farces in scarlet, bismuth pink, Reckitt's blue, orange, with perhaps spaces in yellow, intended to indicate daffodils or tulips, placed in jugs, the 'drawing' of which any Board school child would be ashamed of. Is it for nothing that Italian, Flemish, Spanish, and British masters have worked in reverses, sparing neither toil nor time in producing perfection in every detailed line and touch? They worked with no mercenary motive, and were content to earn for their masterpieces sums of two figures. Now we are gravely told the perpetrators of these practical jokes ask and get what would have seemed a fortune to a Dürer, a Raeburn, and a Reynolds. It is tragic, but remediable."

John Duncan, by then an Associate Member of the R.S.A. leapt to Bunty's defence. In response to another attack on his friend's 'Bolshevik' paintings, this time by the Professor of Art, Baldwin Brown, he wrote:

"There is no arguing about Art, which is, after all, a matter of sensibility. As Professor Baldwin Brown can see no artistic value or interest in Mr Cadell's present exhibits, I can only conclude that he is insensitive to qualities of a high order that many people gifted with that same sense find beautiful."

The controversy continued almost every day until February 6th when Bunty himself sent a wonderfully brief note to the original complainant.

"Mr Cadell presents his compliments to Lady Constance Emmott and begs to thank her for the free advertisement she has so generously given him".

The paintings that aroused so much attention were vividly coloured still life works, two of which were sold in the Society of Eight Exhibition. In style, these and later works were wholly different from the impressionistic paintings which Bunty had produced between 1910 and 1915. Instead, as illustrated in Plates 44 & 46, there were boldly defined patterns

Plate 44

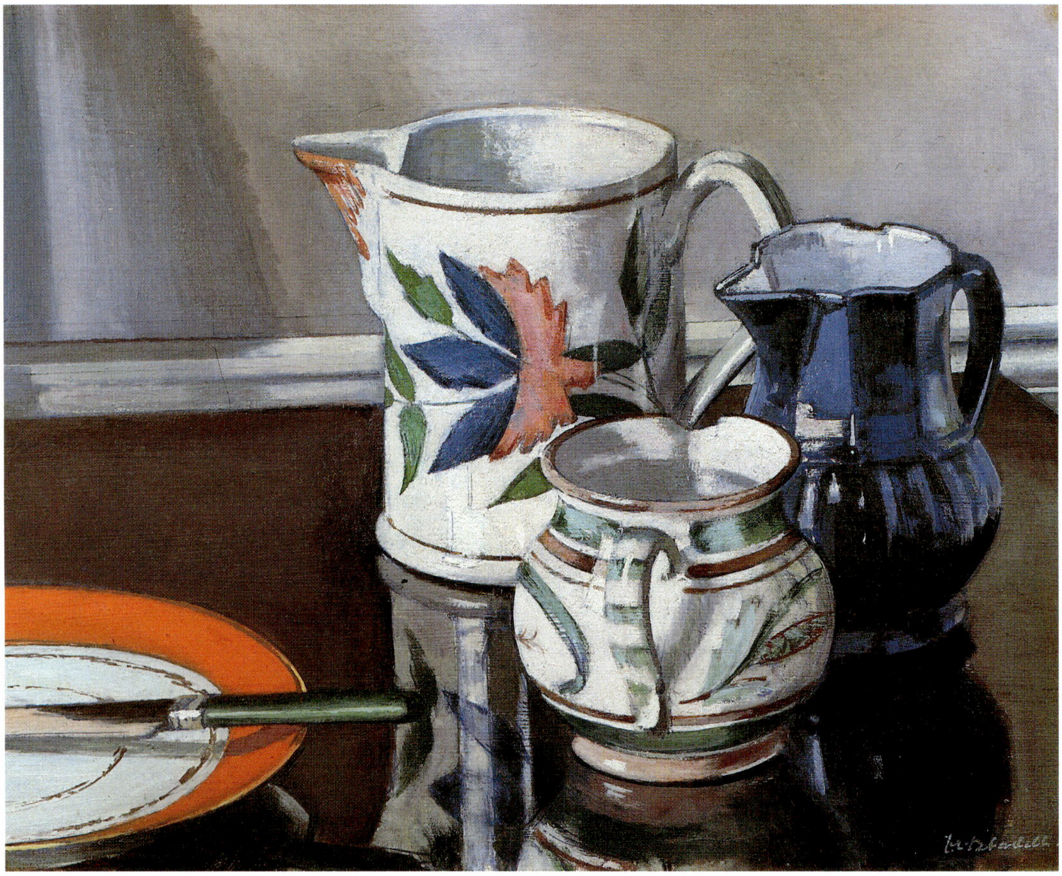

The Red Plate, c. 1925 oil 15 × 18 in.

of strong, bright colour which gave the paintings a tighter structure. This style was equally pronounced in the delightfully crisp, powerful interiors that he painted during the following twelve years at 6 Ainslie Place.

Every summer Bunty forsook the considerable comfort of his Edinburgh studio for the rather more basic conditions on Iona. By 1920, he had arranged to rent a cottage on the island and Peploe joined him there for an extended stay. It was Peploe's first visit to Iona, and its beauty and challenging subject matter ensured his frequent return. Both artists painted together regularly. Peploe had a special liking for the north end of the island with its spectacular view across the brilliant white sands in the foreground to the north end of Mull on the horizon.

Bunty's Iona paintings were less controversial than the bright still lifes that he had shown in the earlier part of the year, and received a better public reception when he returned to Edinburgh with them. With an eye towards a future exhibition, Alexander Reid purchased seven views of Iona, with another twelve selling to various of Bunty's patrons who came to visit him in his magnificent new home in the heart of the fashionable Georgian 'New Town' district of the city.

There was no mistaking the house in Ainslie Place in which Bunty lived. He painted the front door in vivid ultramarine. Inside, he occupied the bottom half of the house; there was a

Plate 45

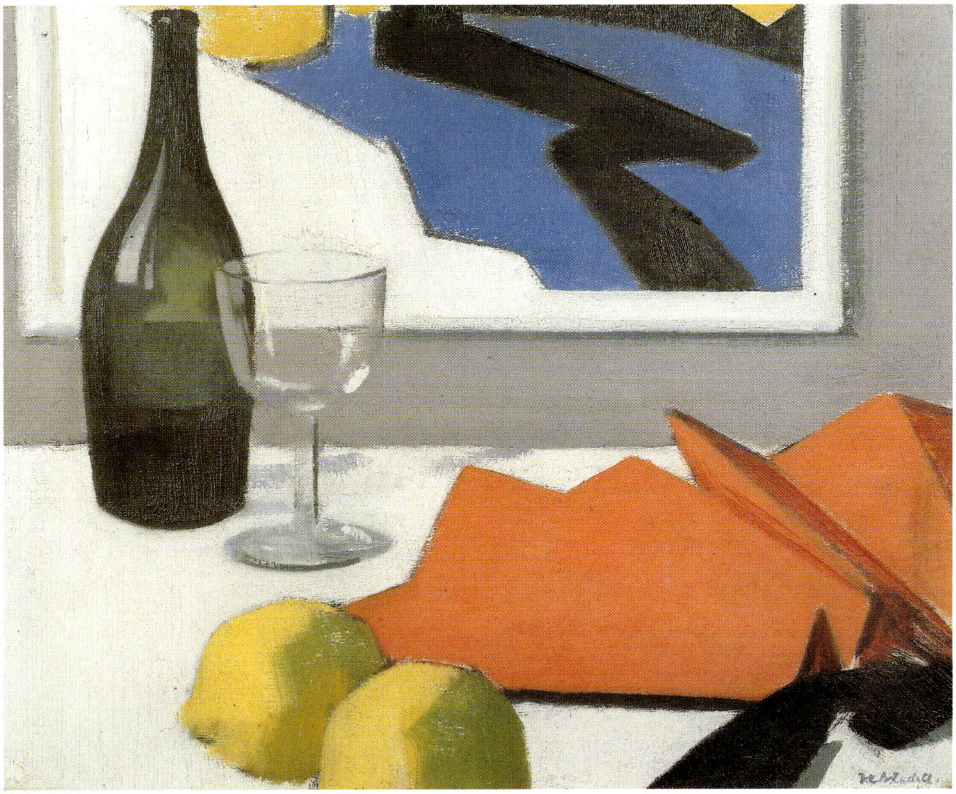

The Red Fan, c. 1923 oil 15 × 18 in.

Plate 46

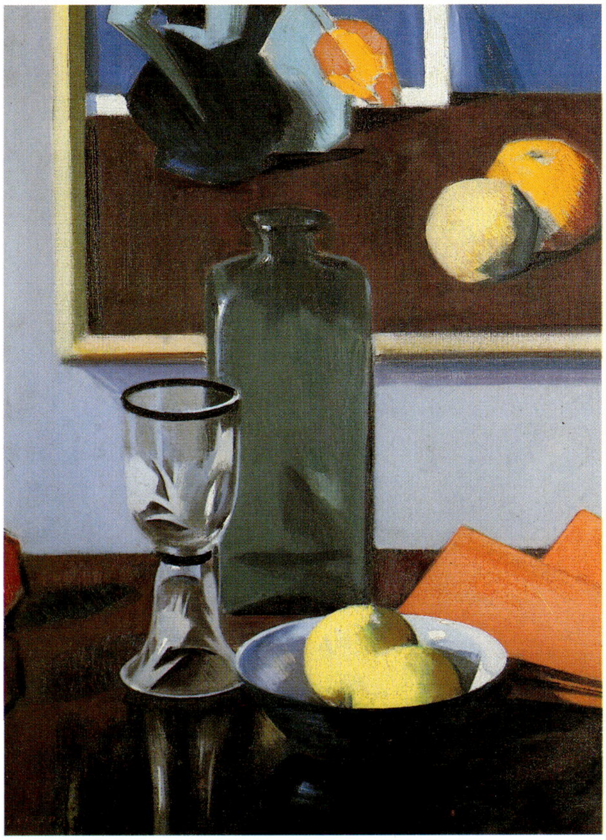

The Green Bottle, c. 1927 oil 24 × 18 in.

Plate 47

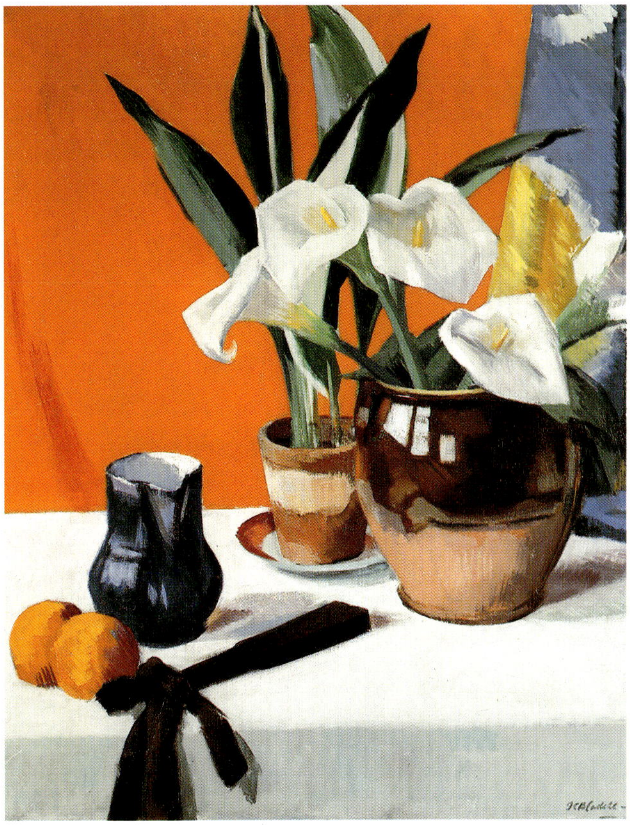

Arum Lillies, c. 1924 oil 36 × 28 in.

billiards table in the basement and ample storage space. The main rooms, on the ground floor, were large and well proportioned. He used the drawing room as his studio, and painted the walls a rich mauve colour in sharp contrast to the brilliant white painted woodwork of the panelled, inter-connecting doors. The highly polished dark wooden floor, reflected the bright colours of the carefully placed Whytock and Reid furniture and provided the theme for many of his more dramatic interiors.

Bunty was meticulous in ensuring that his studio was always tidy. When he had finished painting, his palette would be cleaned and put away together with the other materials; finished and unfinished works were stored in an orderly fashion. In many ways this was a reflection of Bunty's belief in the beauty of well ordered and cleanly structured surroundings, a view that was shared by his man-servant Charles Oliver.

Charles had served in the navy during the war and was taken on by Bunty soon afterwards. The early years of his employment were ones of reasonable prosperity for Bunty; Charles was an excellent cook, waited at table, looked after the studio, and occasionally even negotiated the sale of Bunty's paintings to regular patrons when his master was away. He also modelled for Bunty. It was a measure of Charles' loyalty and the close personal relationship which he developed with his master that he remained in Bunty's employment through the lean years of the early 1930's when there was insufficient income to pay his wages.

However, in the prosperous years of the 1920's Charles' wages were not a problem for Bunty. Of more difficulty was his relationship with the Royal Scottish Academy. He had been nominated for election as an Associate of the R.S.A. in 1918, and again in 1920. On both occasions other artists had been elected ahead of him. On hearing that he had been turned down for a second time, he suffered a momentary loss of temper and declared:

"I shall consent to have my name on the Nomination List again when the President leads the whole Council crawling on their hands and knees round Ainslie Place to my door, with olive branches gripped between their teeth".

Bunty then withdrew his name from the Nomination List. His subsequent request to have his paintings removed from the R.S.A annual exhibition was rejected and led to a three year period when he refused to enter any works for the show. Similarly, apart from entering paintings for the annual Society of Eight exhibition, he did not participate in any other shows in Edinburgh until 1930.

Instead, Bunty developed a close working relationship with Alexander Reid of Glasgow whose son, A. J. McNeill Reid, organised an exhibition of Bunty's works at Warneuke's Gallery on Sauchiehall Street early in 1921. It was an outstanding success. Ten paintings sold, the majority of which were 'new style' still life works, four on large canvasses. William Russell-Flint was staying in Helensburgh at the time and wrote to Bunty on January 13th.

"I had the pleasure today of seeing your exhibition and am making so bold as to send you my hearty congratulations. It is a most refreshing and delightful show. You have struck a pleasantly sane modern note which is very enjoyable after the advanced trash one gets so tired of in London and Paris. Your henchman at the Gallery told me that you were one of two artists in Scotland. I hope there really are more but if there is only the one other he certainly hasn't a look in!"

There was a similar reaction from another artist, W. Y. Macgregor, the 'father' of the Glasgow School, who wrote to Bunty after seeing his three exhibits (*'Interior'*, *'The Buddha'*, *'Portrait of a Lady in Black'*) at the R.G.I. Exhibition in the autumn. He wrote:

Plate 48

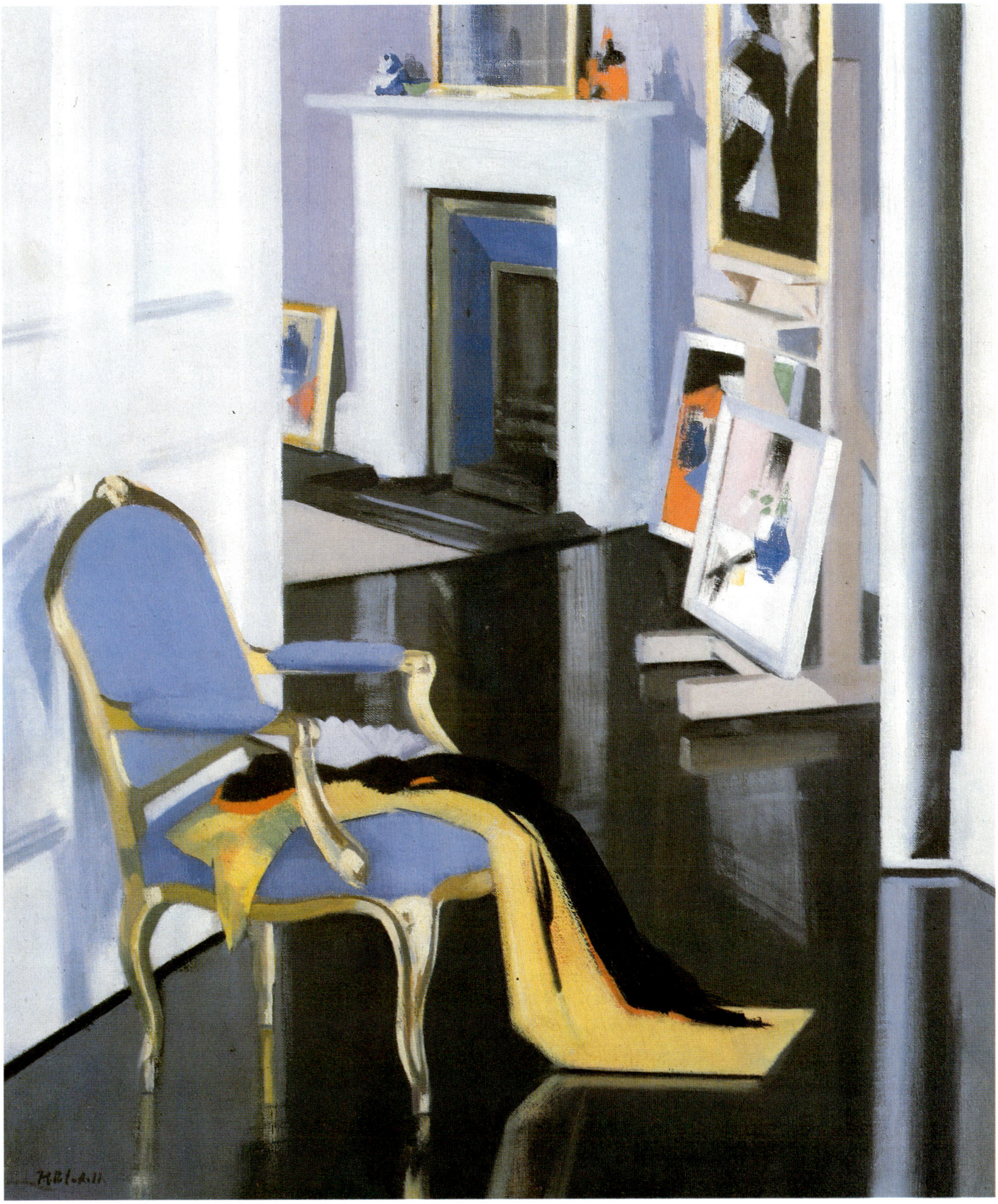

The Gold Chair, 1921 oil 24 × 20 in.

Plate 49

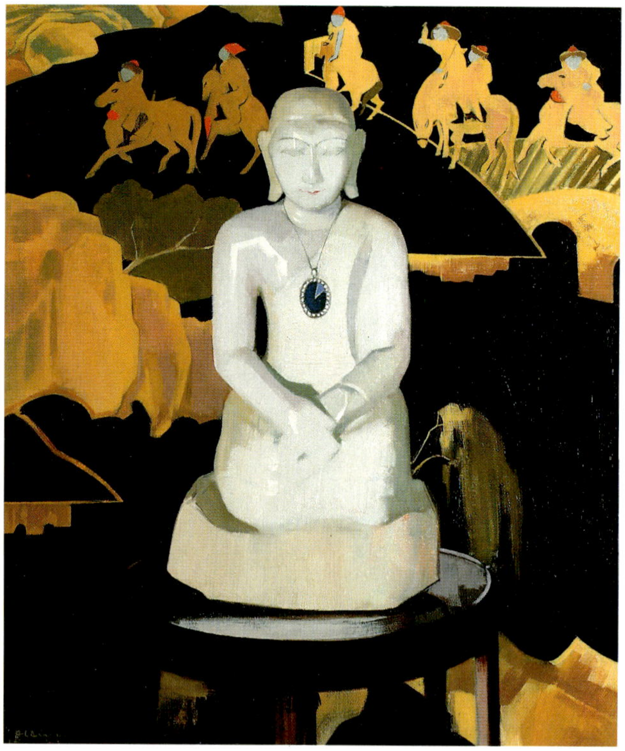

Buddha, Black and Gold, c. 1921

oil 30 × 25 in.

"Your portrait is capital and also your '*Buddha*'. I think they are the best pictures you have painted and I must congratulate you on the distinguished appearance you make in the Glasgow show".

Admiration from other artists was obviously welcome, but it did not sell paintings, and it was in these early years at Ainslie Place that G. W. Service's patronage really contributed greatly to Bunty's success. During 1921 he purchased fourteen paintings, mainly views of Iona, but also one large interior entitled '*The Eagle Mirror*'. However, perhaps the most impressive interior that was painted at this time was the view of his studio entitled '*The Gold Chair*' (Plate 48); it was sold in late October 1921 at an exhibition in Dundee.

It was Bunty's normal practice to bring back all his unsold paintings from Iona at the end of his annual summer stay so that he had works available for sale in the winter and spring of the following year. The standard size panels, which measured just under fifteen by eighteen inches, normally sold for between thirty and thirty-five pounds each, though Bunty was always likely to amend the price depending on the purchaser. The price of his larger works, which were normally painted on canvas, depended entirely on Bunty's view of their quality and how he was feeling at the time; in some instances, the price of a particular painting would change from day to day.

Early in 1922 George Service purchased three large canvasses, and subsequently nine 'standard' size panels of Iona. One of the larger works was '*Interior, Iona Cathedral*' (Plate 50). This painting helps to highlight Bunty's ability to recreate both the atmosphere and texture of his subject matter – in this case the coolness of the church interior together with the almost absorbent texture of the stonework. George Service's support continued to play a

Plate 50

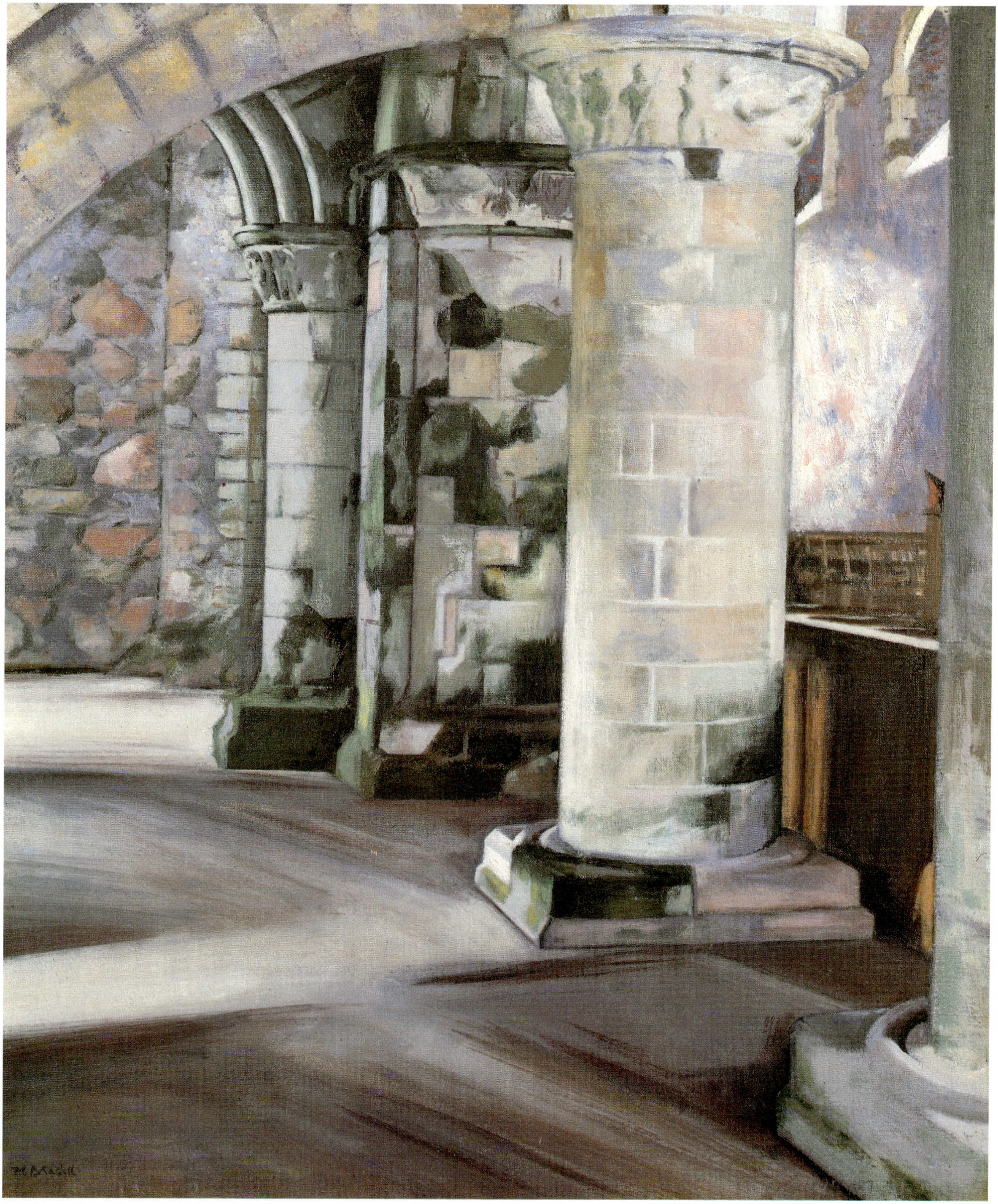

Interior, Iona Cathedral, 1922 oil 30 × 20 in.

Plate 51

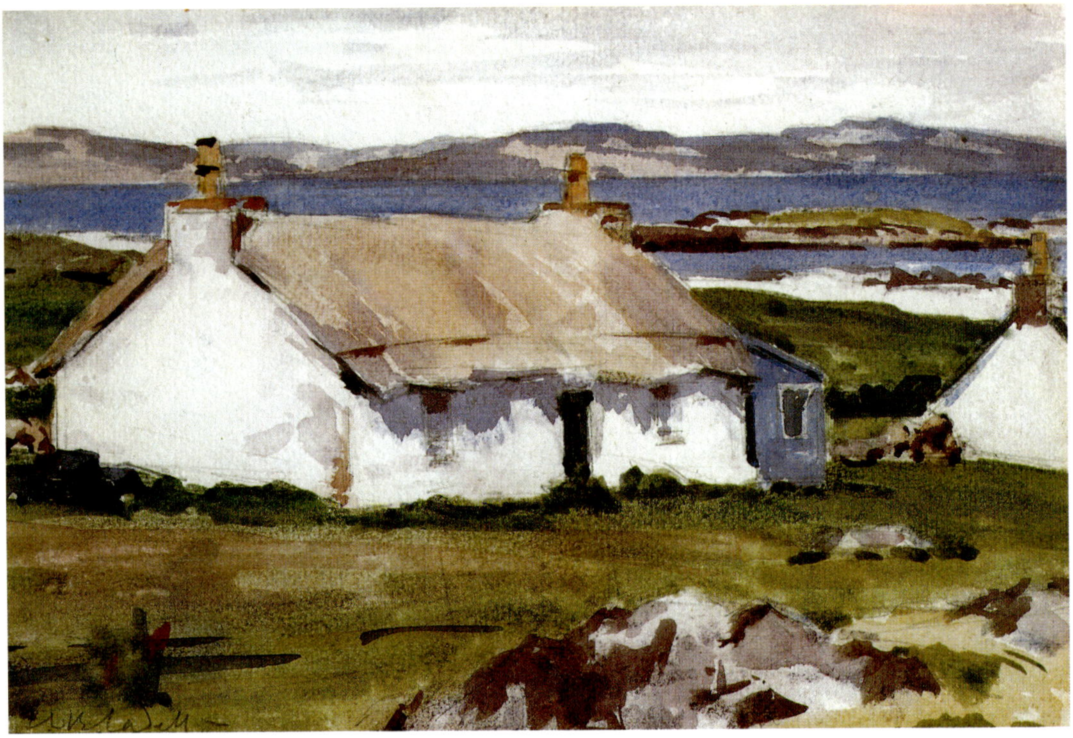

Iona Croft, c. 1926 watercolour 7 × 10 in.

Plate 52

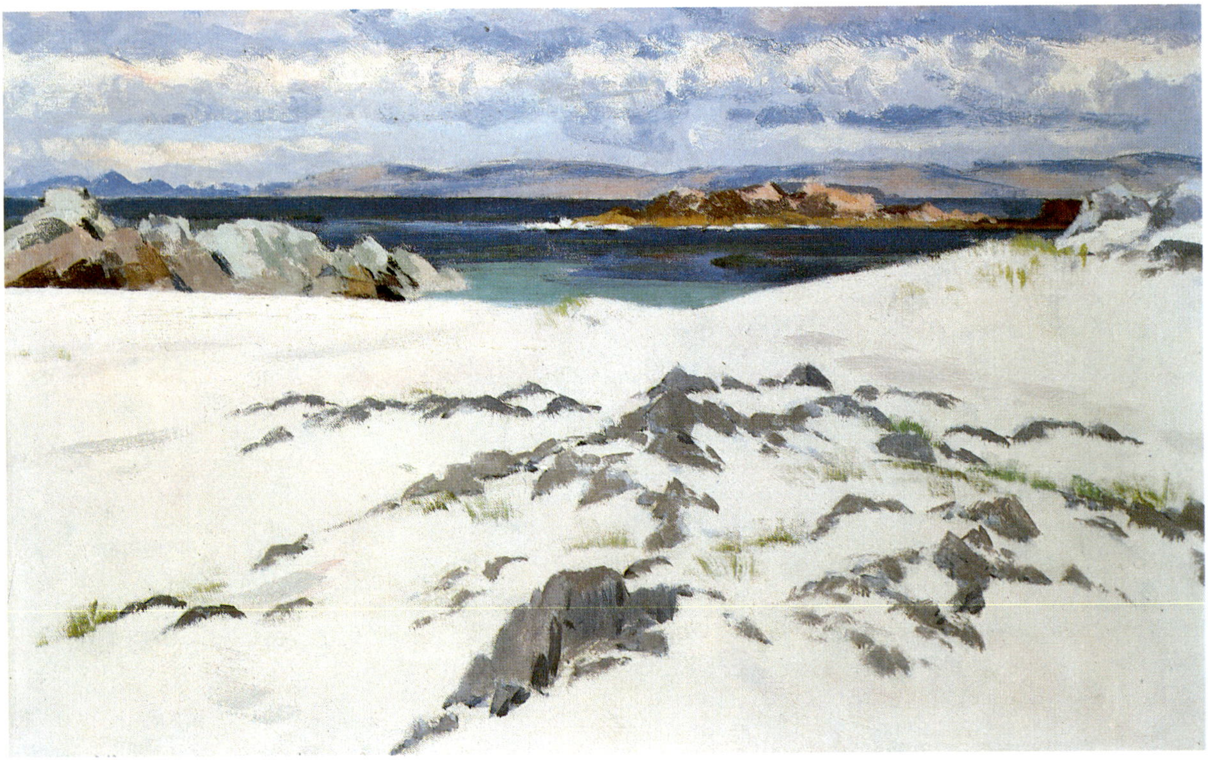

Iona, c. 1922 oil 20 × 30 in.

Plate 53

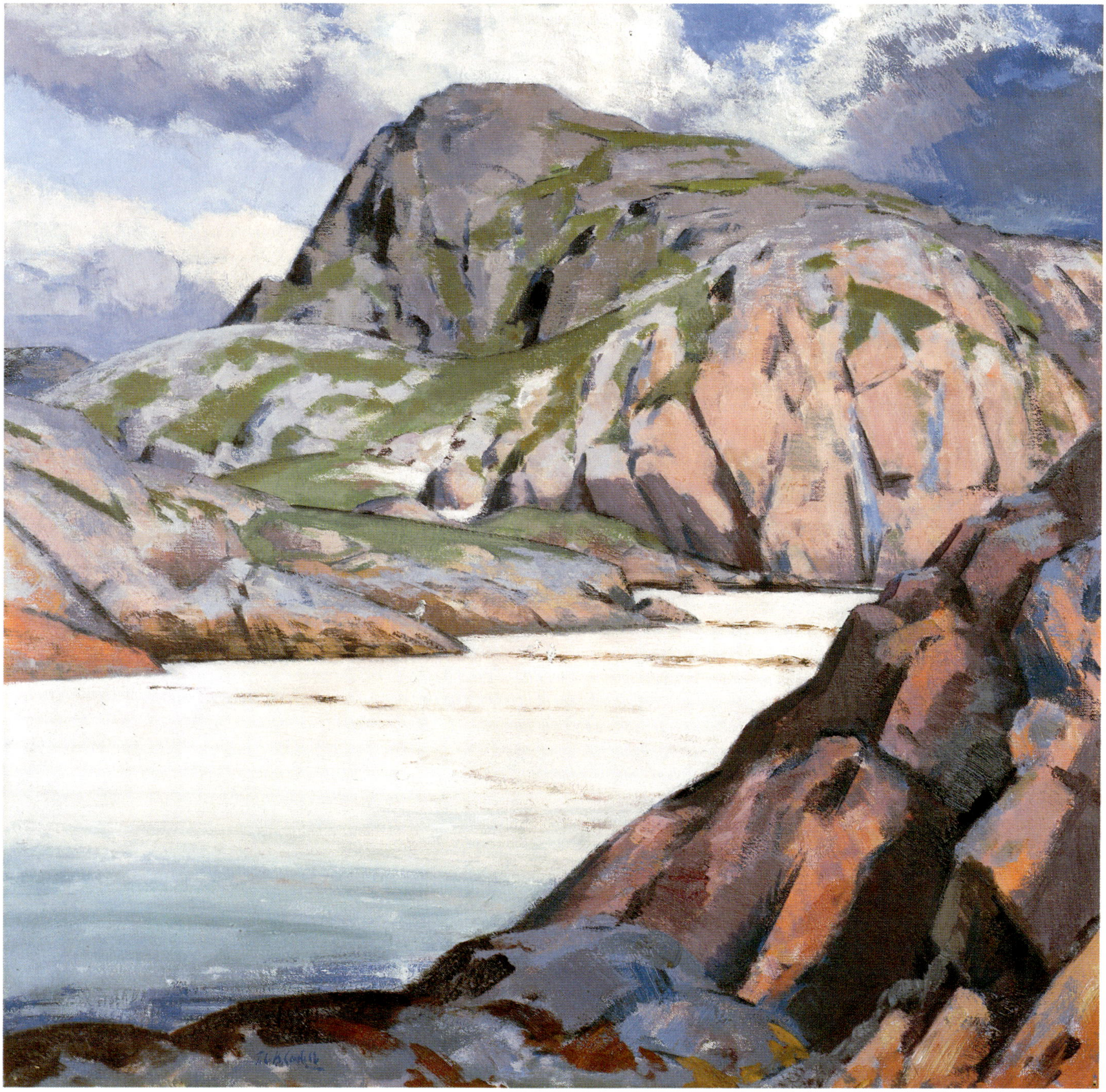

Port Bhan, 1926

oil 30 × 30 in.

major part in Bunty's prosperity for the next six years. For, although numerous paintings sold, the number of purchasers was relatively small.

When only two paintings sold at the second exhibition at Warneuke's Gallery in Glasgow in March 1922, it was not only a disappointment for Bunty but also a cause for some concern from a financial standpoint. In need of extra funds, he wrote to Reid in Glasgow, asking him to purchase a painting that Peploe had given him. Reid replied by return.

TEL. No. CENTRAL 8687.

ALEX. REID

(LA SOCIÉTÉ DES BEAUX-ARTS).

GLASGOW: 117 & 121 WEST GEORGE STREET
AND AT PARIS.

117 & 121 WEST GEORGE STREET,
GLASGOW. 19th.Apr.1922.

F. C. B. Cadell Esq.
6 Ainslie Place,
Edinburgh.

Dear Mr Cadell,

My father is at present in bed with a cold and has asked me to reply to your letter of 17th. inst. regarding the picture by Peploe.

Both my father and myself like this picture very much, but the price is quite out of the question. No picture by Peploe has ever, to our knowledge, brought a price anything approaching £150 and it would be impossible for us to get that for it, let alone give it. We would be willing to give £80 and chance it at that if you care, but could not give any more.

I met Peploe in Edinburgh about a fortnight ago and he told me that you were feeling the better of your holiday. I hope you have completely recovered your normal health, and are able once more to resume your painting.

With kindest regards,

Yours sincerely,

A. J. McNeill Reid.

Bunty was in no position to negotiate and reluctantly parted with the Peploe still life to Reid for eighty pounds on 25th April.

About six weeks later he left for Iona. By then, there was a regular group of artists who visited the island in summer, among them William Mervyn Glass, John Duncan, and Peploe. Living in a croft (Plate 51), but a frequent visitor to the St. Columba Hotel, Bunty's engaging personality and irrespressible sense of humour made him the natural focal point for their meeting. His distinctive style of dress (he always wore a kilt, usually with a bright waistcoat, and a tam o'shanter) ensured that he was instantly recognisable from afar. The islanders regarded him with genuine fondness, and the younger ones with a respect reserved

Plate 54

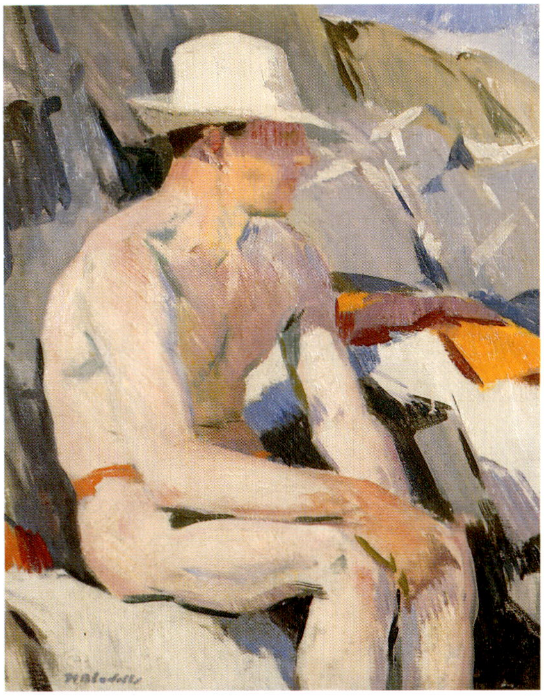

The Bather, c. 1923 oil 18 × 15 in.

Plate 55

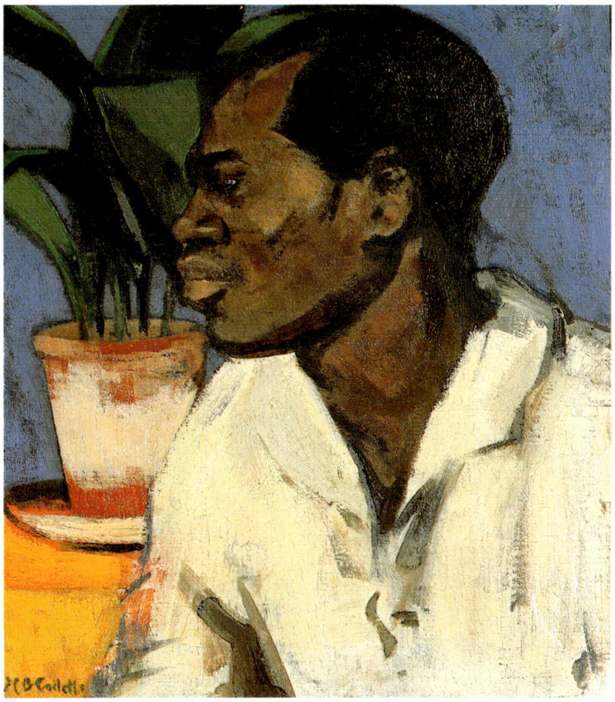

The Negro, 1922 oil 18 × 16 in.

for someone of great character. It is said that, on one occasion, two small boys were studying the imposing sight of Bunty approaching in full highland dress. One turned to the other and asked, "Who is that man?" to which his friend replied, "That's not a man, that's Mr Cadell!"

Having such a close relationship with the island community, it was always a wrench to return to Edinburgh; however, by the end of August Bunty was back in Ainslie Place. The autumn and early winter months were highly successful; twenty-nine paintings of Iona were sold, together with three still life works, two interiors and his first version of *'The Negro'* (Plate 55).

With the security of some money in the bank, Bunty made plans to visit the south of France in the spring of 1923. This was after his first London exhibition, a joint show at the Leicester Galleries in February featuring his works and those of Peploe and Hunter. Bunty entered thirty works. Comparing them to earlier examples of his paintings, the Daily Mail commented:

"Mr Cadell was apt to leave his pictures in a state of summary sketchiness which amounted to flippancy. He has solidified his style. All forms are stated with an assurance that carries conviction. He has passed from vague impression to architectoric organisation".

The Times voiced the opinion that:

"Mr Cadell is much smoother (than Leslie Hunter) and his colour schemes are of a simpler daring in contrast".

Plate 56

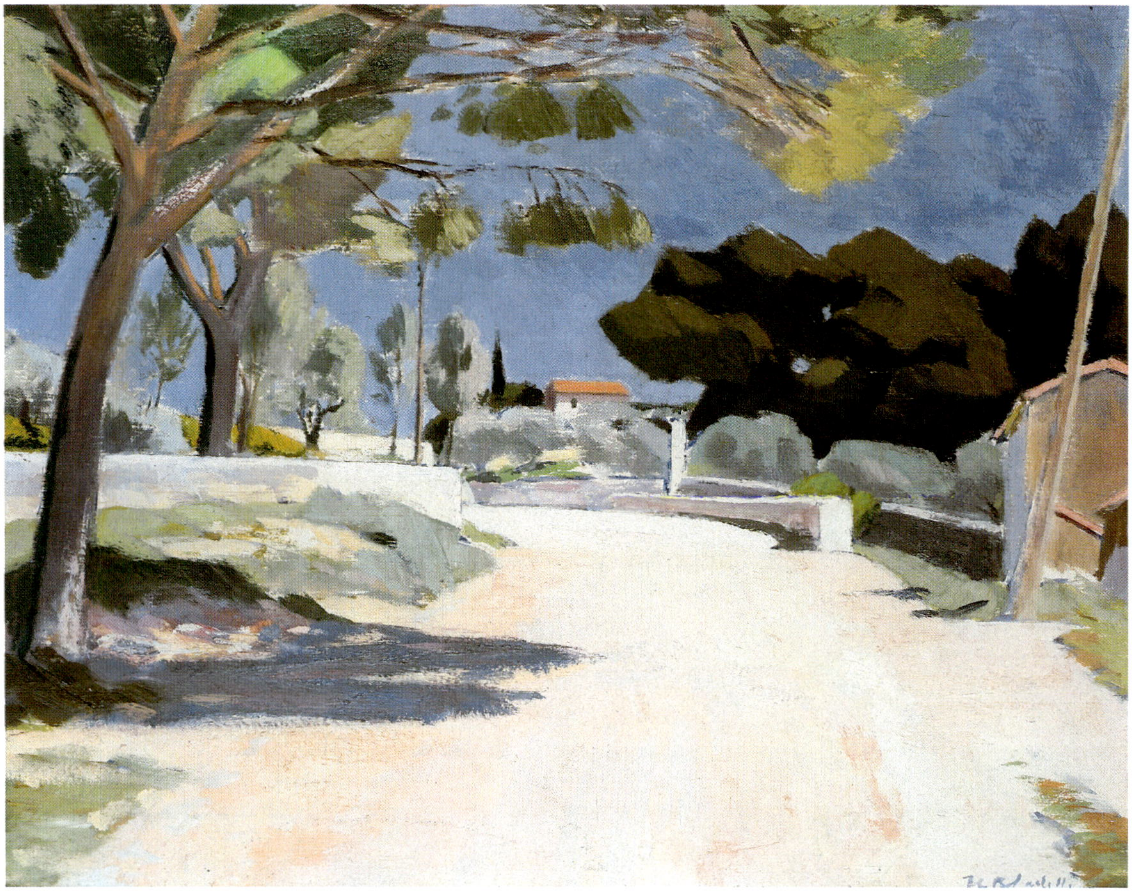

Cassis, 1923/24 oil 15 × 18 in.

The Sunday Observer also reviewed the exhibition, commenting that:

"Mr Cadell follows him (Peploe) so closely, both in colour and subject matter that it would be hard to distinguish between the two were it not that Mr Cadell's emphasis of design leans him towards the two-dimensional . . . he has gained conspicously in his solidity of handling. There was a time when he took things a little too easily and relied to heavily on the charms of his gay palette – when his pictures were clever suggestions . . . which left too much to be filled in by the spectator's plastic imagination. Not a trace of the earlier Cadell is left . . . although his colour has lost none of its charm and harmonious brightness".

There was general critical approval for Bunty's new 'solidity' of handling, but only five of his paintings sold and Alexander Reid purchased all of them for inclusion in his Cadell Exhibition in Glasgow in May 1923. It was one of the least successful shows that Reid ever held, and, although he had other exhibitions of Bunty's work, there is no record of his purchasing more than the occasional painting directly from Bunty again.

The loss of direct support of such an influential dealer had an almost immediate impact on Bunty's fortunes. However, it did not prevent him from visiting the south of France in the spring of 1923, and again the following year. On the recommendation of Peploe, who had

Plate 57

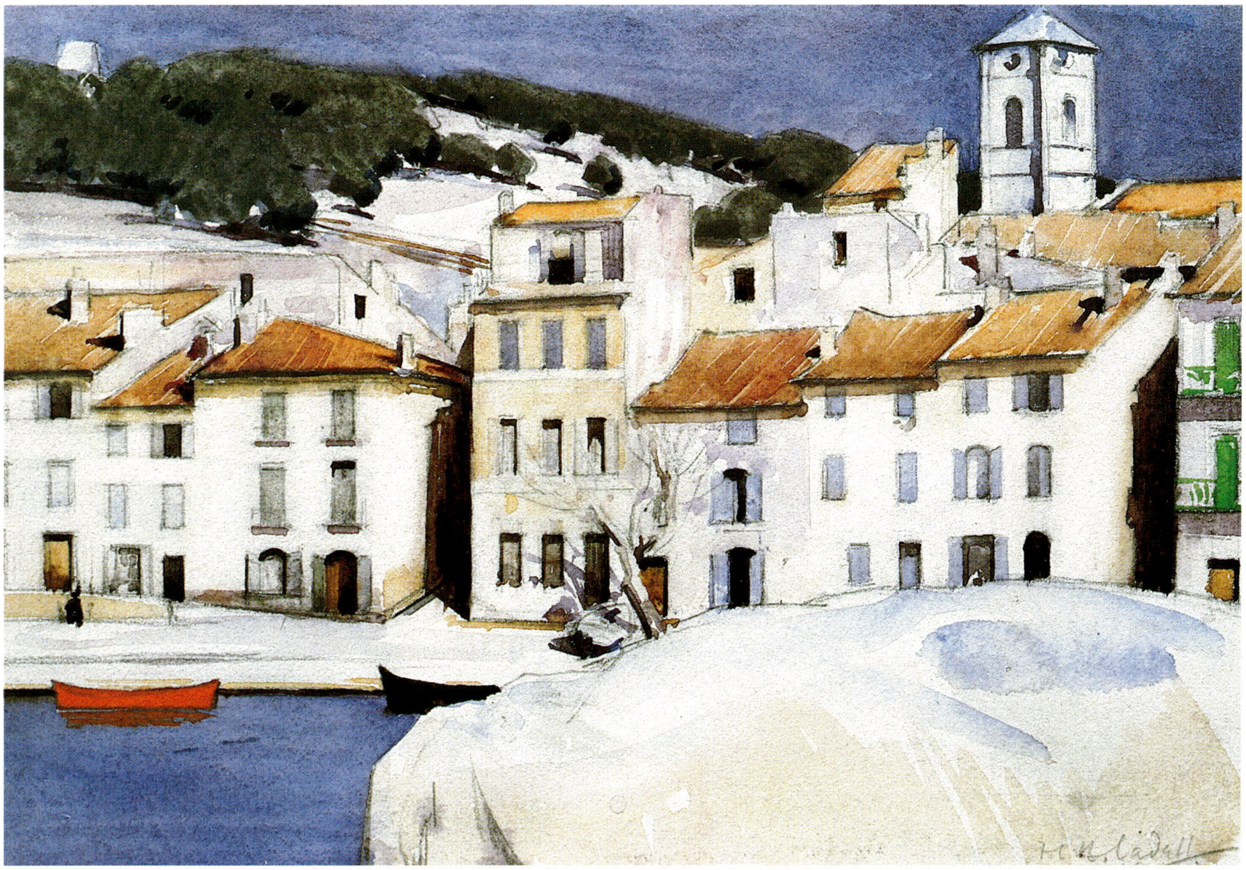

Cassis, the Habour, 1923 watercolour 7 × 10 in.

stayed there in 1913, he stayed at the Hotel Panorama in Cassis, a small fishing port not far from Marseilles. The vividly coloured houses on the waterfront and the open rolling countryside in the hills above the village, were natural subject matter for Bunty who produced some of his most inspired work of the period, (Plates 56-58).

The paintings were well received in Edinburgh; the use of bright colours and strong, solid lines seemed to many to be more understandable and acceptable in these French landscape paintings than in the still life works produced in his Ainslie Place studio around the same time. G. W. Service purchased four Cassis panels, and five more sold before the end of the year; various other paintings, mainly of Iona, were also sold but it obviously worried Bunty that his work did not have more widespread appeal and that his main supporter among the dealers was no longer anxious to buy work outright.

Bunty's reaction was to send over thirty works for sale at auction during 1924. Three were sold at Dowells in Edinburgh in February, nine in May, and fifteen in July. Edmiston's in Glasgow sold three in May and another three in June. In most cases the paintings achieved only a quarter of their retail price.

Bunty returned to Cassis in April 1924 in the company of Peploe. He stayed in France for several months probably attending the exhibition held at Galerie Barbazangues in Paris from June 2nd to 15th entitled 'Les Peintres de L'Ecosse Moderne'. Bearing in mind the influence

Plate 58

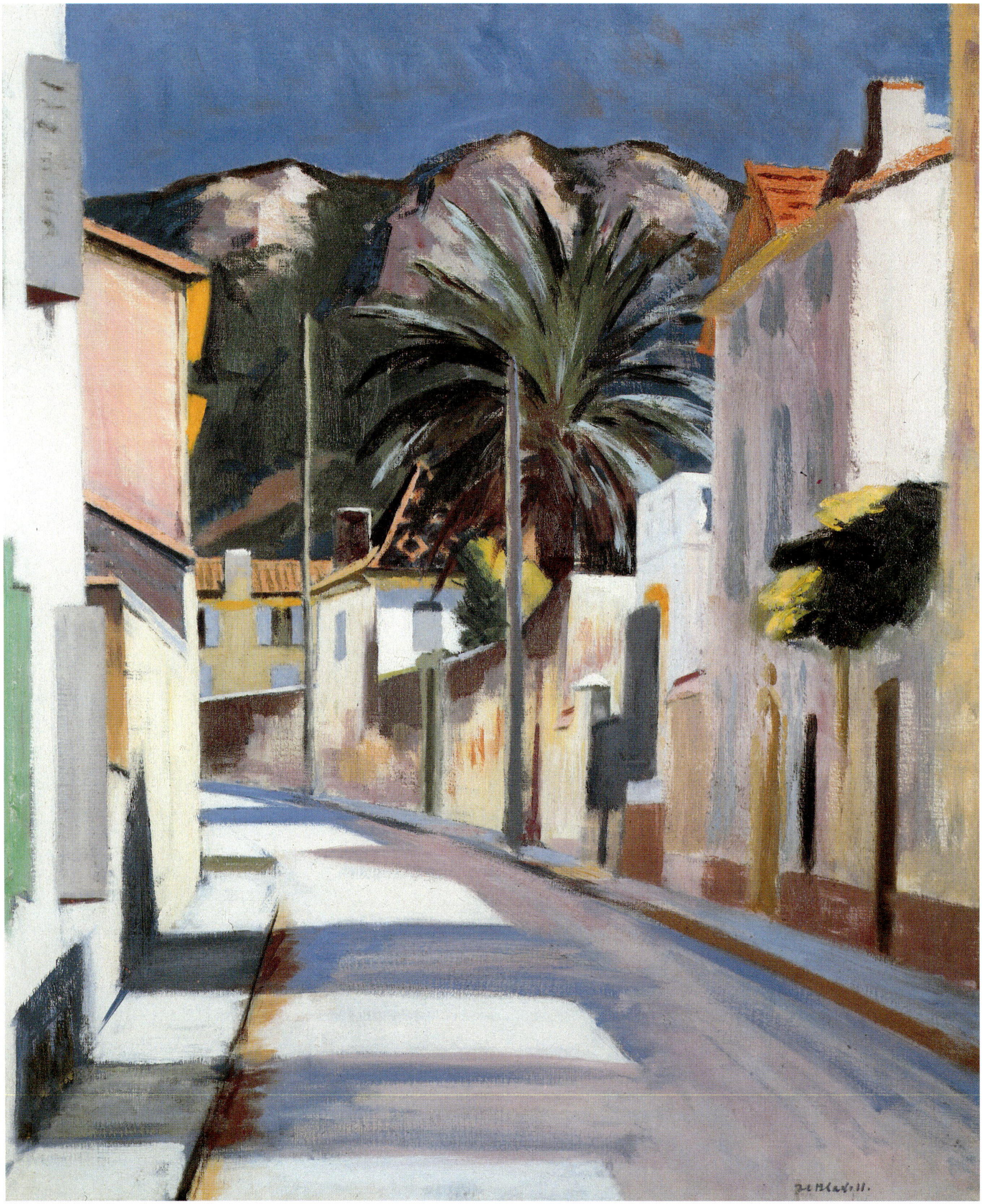

Cassis, 1923/24 oil 30 × 25 in.

Plate 59

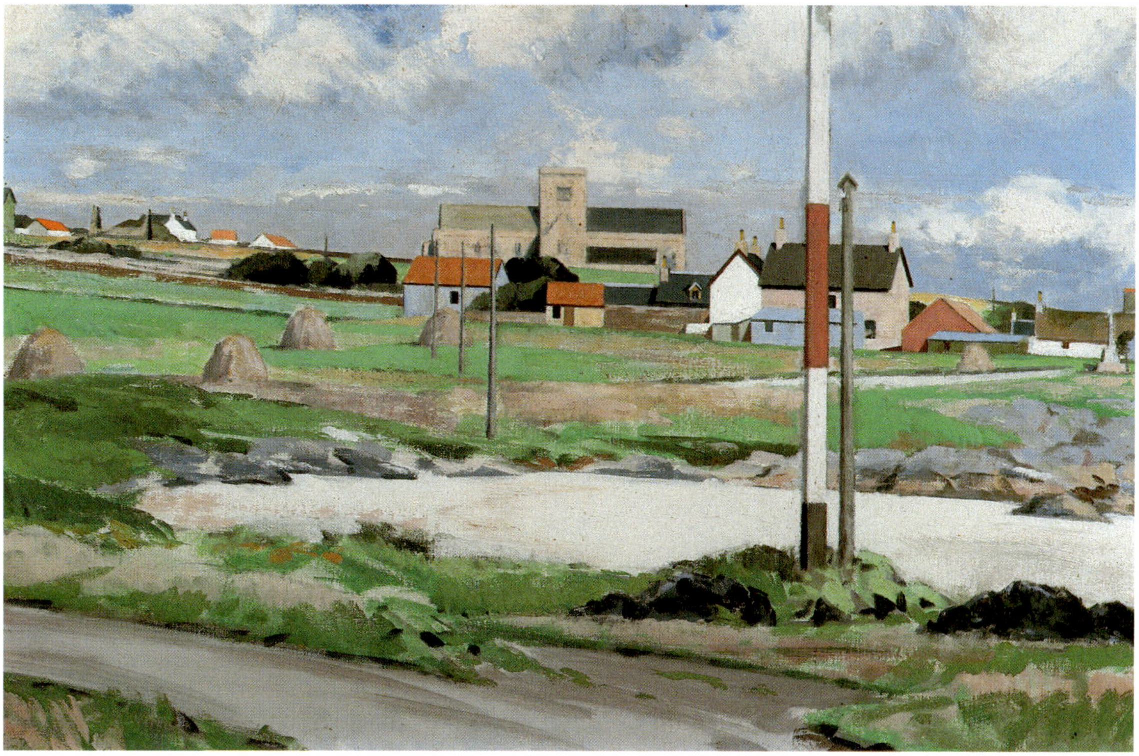

The Village of Iona, 1926 oil 20 × 30 in.

that France had exerted on the careers of all four artists, it was fitting that Paris should stage the first show devoted entirely to the works of Peploe, Cadell, Hunter and Fergusson.

The following year the Leicester Galleries in London held an exhibition by the same four artists. Among the works that Bunty showed were three of the Cassis paintings that he had produced the previous year. In an all too familiar story, the show received good critical acclaim but not one of Bunty's paintings sold. Instead, fifteen more were consigned for sale to the auction houses where together they made a few shillings over fify pounds. The relative lack of success was happily not allowed to interfere too much with Bunty's way of life and although it was now usual for the account with his butcher to be settled by the gift of a painting, the dinner parties (with Charles acting as butler) continued much as before.

Towards the end of the year, Bunty received a visit from A. J. McNeill Reid, who purchased only one painting, a still life entitled, '*Pink Azalea*'. When he sold it three year later, it was the first of Bunty's paintings to be purchased by Ion Harrison who became his greatest patron during the 1930's. It was one of the few still life works that Bunty produced that year. Instead, he spent considerable time on Iona. As he painted quickly, the water-colours and panels mounted up in the little croft. While Bunty went out to paint, Charles was left inside to welcome those who came to try and acquire a 'Bunty Cadell' of Iona. Charles used to greet all such visitors with enthusiasm. However, a different mood prevailed when negotiations had been concluded, with those purchasing a work being shown out

Plate 60

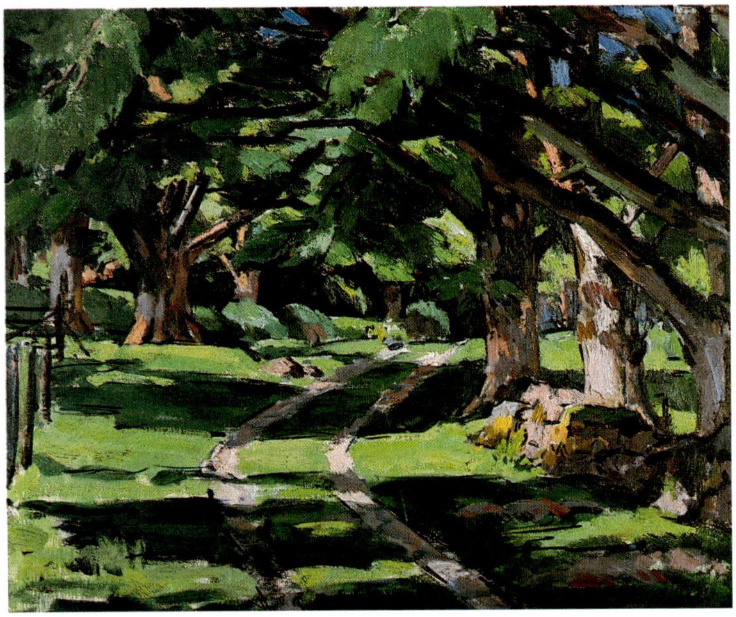

Auchnacraig, c. 1927 oil 25 × 30 in.

through the front door with great ceremony, while those who did not, had to make do with the back.

One of the most powerful large canvasses of Iona which he painted during this period was '*Port Bhan*' (Plate 53). It was sold in Edinburgh at the beginning of 1926. Eighty-two other Iona paintings found buyers during the year. It must have been an extraordinary and rather unhappy sight to see an artist of Bunty's quality having to stimulate business by organising a 'half price' sale, but one was held at his studio between 25th March and 3rd April. Various other small exhibitions were held during the year, including another at 6 Ainslie Place in mid December. However, an undoubted high-spot during the year was the Corporation of Glasgow's acquisition of '*A Lady in Black*' (Plate 63) for the Kelvingrove Art Gallery. It was the first public collection to acquire a major work by Cadell.

The following year, Bunty again spent the summer months on Iona. On the way to the island, he visited Auchnacraig on the east coast of Mull for the first time, and completed several distinctive paintings of the surrounding countryside. The paintings illustrated in Plates 60 & 73 are typical of the work produced on this and subsequent visits.

However, during the year, it was becoming increasingly clear to Bunty that he was not able to continue to live his existing lifestyle on his modest income as an artist. By the end of the year, he had resolved to sell his house and a few months later wrote to G. W. Service, explaining:

"I have sold my house to Ramage and am in the act of moving into his flat. A great upheaval! Nearly all the valuable furniture in this house I have sent to Christie's in London for sale and am glad to say that . . . the head man thinks that my things ought to fetch a very good price and I hope that they may".

As Ramage already occupied the top two floors of 6 Ainslie Place, the move was not as traumatic as it might have been. The rooms of the new flat were well proportioned and it was from this new studio that Bunty produced some striking and powerful examples of his talent.

Plate 61

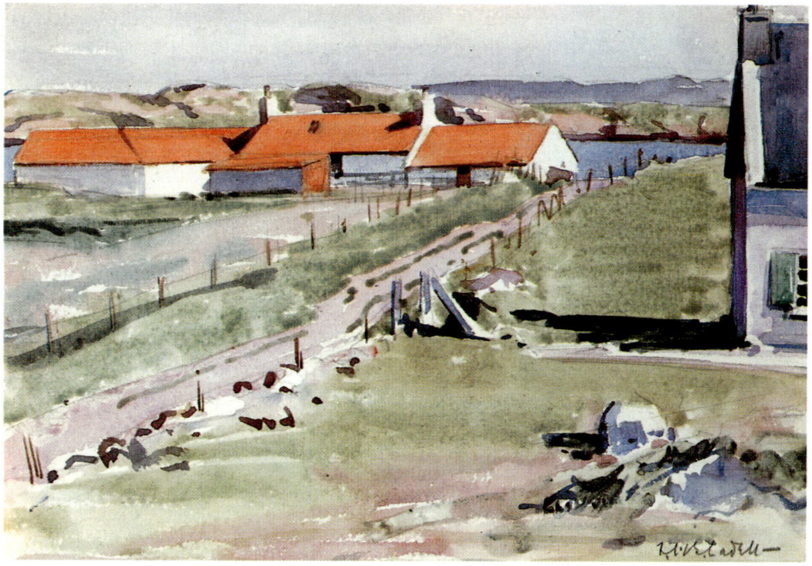

Red Roofs, Iona, c. 1925 watercolour 10 × 14 in.

Plate 62

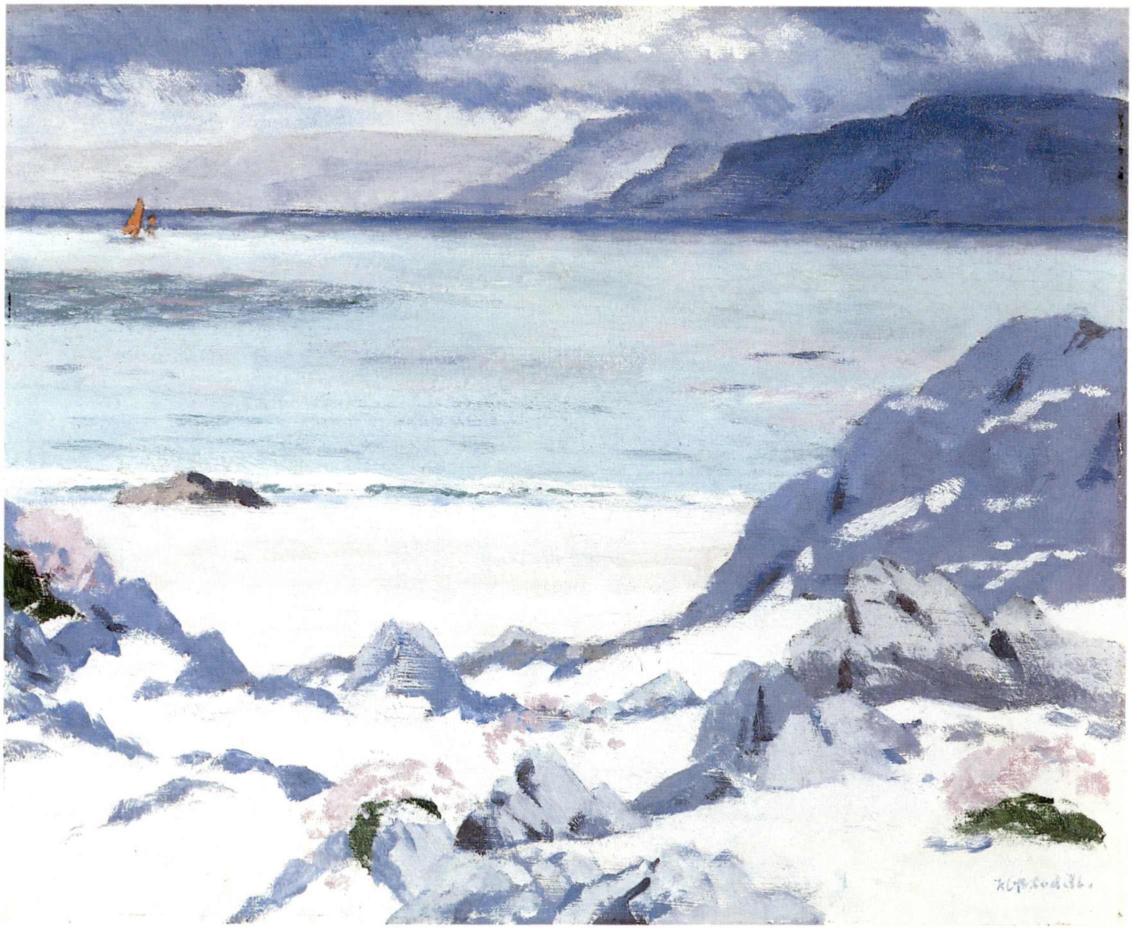

Iona, 1926 oil 15 × 18 in.

Plate 63

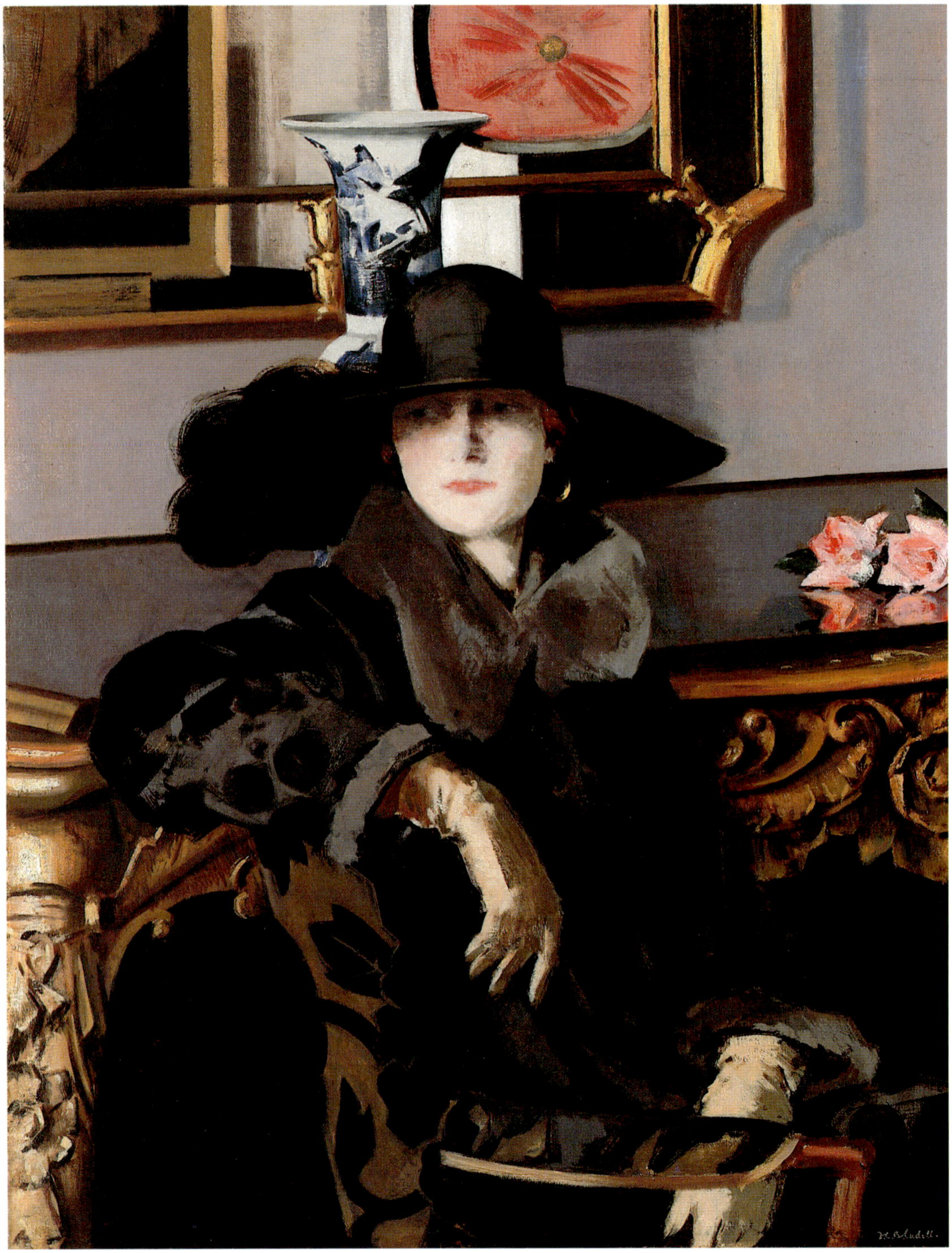

A Lady in Black, c. 1926 oil 40 × 30 in.

Chapter Five

1928–1932

The seven years that Bunty lived in the main rooms of 6 Ainslie Place were probably the happiest of his life. Just prior to his move to the rather more cramped quarters on the second floor, he, or rather Charles, acquired a cat which provided hours of entertainment. In a letter to his sister dated January 6th 1928 he wrote:

"I have just been attacked by a very fierce girl (i.e. a black and white kate (sic) 6 months old) all black except for white specks on feet . . . and huge yellow-green eyes. Rather attractive! She is rushing like a race-horse backwards and forwards along the whole length of this 60ft room and every now and then advancing sideways with arched back to the attack on my white spats . . . Charles got her when I was away and I arrived from Iona to find her very much at home and the house would seem quite queer without her now."

A piece of paper with sketches of the cat in a variety of 'poses' was enclosed with the letter, and is illustrated (page 98). Charles and the cat moved with Bunty to the new studio in April, 1928. During the move, Bunty received a letter from George Service regarding the possibility of his producing some posters for MacBraynes, the ferry owners who were negotiating a contract for the operation of ferries to the Western Isles. Service wrote:

"It has been pretty well decided to ask you to do three posters. They would suggest one of the Caledonian Canal 40″ × 50″, one of the Iona North End 40″ × 25″, and one of the Gabbart 40″ × 25″. For these three the Directors would be pleased to pay £350. In one of them at least, they would like a steamer to appear . . ."

Bunty's reply was short and to the point.

"I will not be dictated to regarding dimensions: 40″ × 25″ is a size of canvas I would not use on any consideration as, in my opinion it is a bad shape. Iona, North End I will be glad to do but as to the others I will not. I must have a free hand otherwise you must get someone more amenable to discipline to do what you want."

This reaction underlined Bunty's integrity. The possibility of losing a meaningful commission was of little concern in relation to that of compromising his own artistic principles. MacBraynes agreed to his terms and the posters were delivered in September on Bunty's return from Iona. The agreed fee represented approximately half of Bunty's income for the year. The only exhibition that he had that year with a dealer was the one held by Reid in Glasgow in November. It had a depressingly poor result as shown by A. J. McNeill Reid's letter.

The only good news that Bunty received before the end of the year was while staying at Barcaldine Castle in Argyll (Plate 64). It was confirmation that *'The Orange Blind'*, (Plate 1), had been purchased for £150 at the R.G.I. Exhibition by the Trustees of Mr. John Hamil-

TELEPHONE,
CENTRAL 8687.

TELEGRAMS,
"PICTURES, GLASGOW."

ALEX REID & LEFÈVRE, LTD
DEALERS IN WORKS OF ART.

DIRECTORS:
ERNEST A. LEFÈVRE.
A. J. McNEILL REID.
D. M. MACDONALD.

AND AT
1A KING STREET, ST JAMES'S,
LONDON, S.W.1.

117 & 121 WEST GEORGE STREET,
GLASGOW, C.2. 16th Nov., 1928.

F.C.B. Cadell, Esq.,
Barcaldine Castle,
Ledaig, Argyle.

Dear Mr. Cadell,

I have been waiting for several days to summon up enough courage to write you, with what I am afraid is very dismal news. Your Show has, unfortunately, turned out to be the least successful Exhibition I have ever held in our place and the net sales to date amount to £10, received for one water colour drawing. Not many people came in, and these, although they admired the pictures were not to be tempted to purchase. Several transactions that I thought were almost fixed broke down at the last moment and I do not know that there are any chances now of reviving interest in the pictures. Of the customers you sent a note of, the only ones who came in were Colonel Anderson and the Services. Mr. Brown of Greenock sent a note of apology the other day stating that he had been from home and asked me to express to you his apologies.

I do not know what is happening to Glasgow as an Art centre now, whether it is lack of money, or, lack of interest - probably both. Everybody seems to be complaining and the Institute has, I understand, experienced the worst season for many years past. I see that you have been one of the fortunate artists who have sold a picture and I heard in a round-about way that it was being bought for the Corporation.

If you are having a Show in Edinburgh immediately, I will send all the pictures through to Dott, if not, I will send the bulk of them and retain perhaps half a dozen in the chance of doing a little last minute business here.

With kind regards,
Yours sincerely,

A J McNeill Reid

ton, and presented to the City of Glasgow for Kelvingrove Art Gallery. It is, without doubt, one of the most striking Cadell paintings in a public collection.

1929 marked the resumption of a better relationship with the R.S.A. Over the previous eight years he had only entered two paintings for the annual exhibition.

Bunty's relationship with the Royal Glasgow Institute continued to flourish. He exhibited three works in their 1929 exhibition; two elicited the following comments from Frank Rutter of the The Sunday Times:

". . . with its brilliantly vivid colour his interior *'The Open Window'* is a tour-de-force in the luminous rightness of its recession from the breakfast table laid in the foreground to the sunlit garden beyond the window. *'Interior, Summer'* is a further example of Mr. Cadell's dextrous vivacity in vivid illumination."

The third, a large landscape entitled *'The West Highlands'* was the only one to sell and was purchased by Ion Harrison at whose home, Croft House at Helensburgh, Bunty was now a

Plate 64

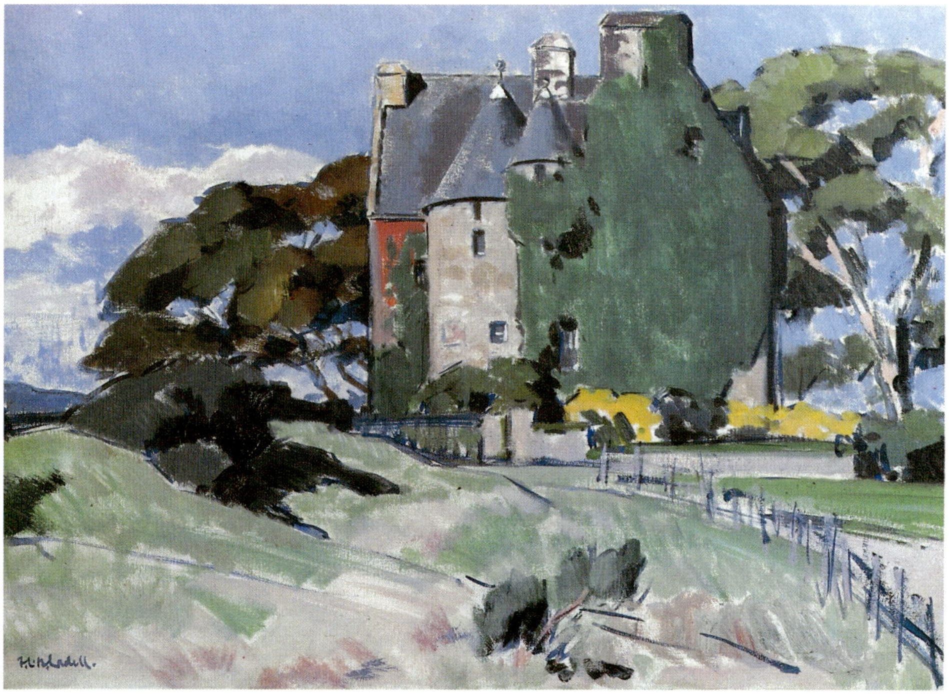

Barcaldine Castle, 1928 oil 22 × 30 in.

Plate 65

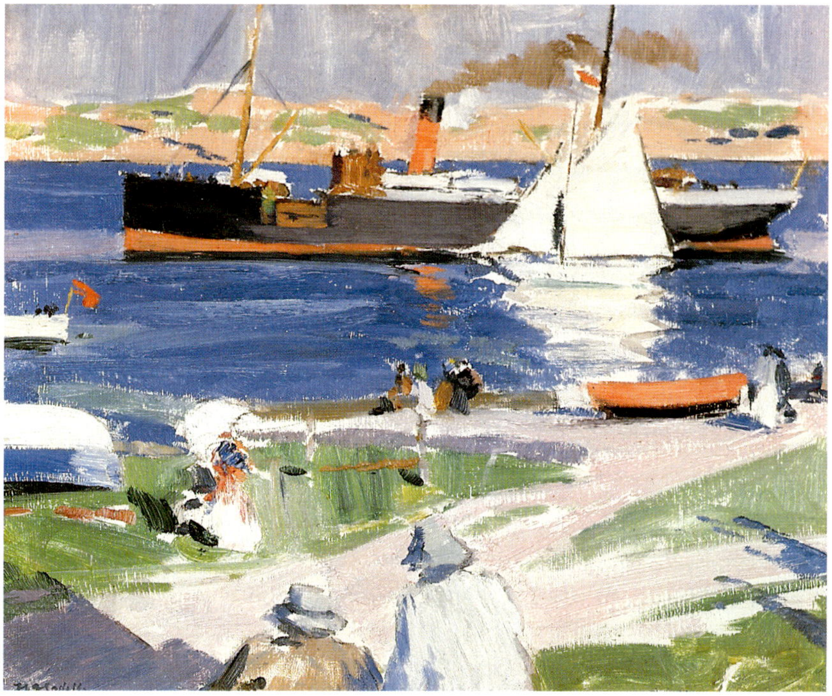

The Dunara Castle, c. 1929 oil 15 × 18 in.

regular and welcome guest. In T. J. Honeyman's book, 'The Three Scottish Colourists', Ion Harrison recalls Bunty's first visit to Croft House.

"He saw, on entering the front door, the '*Pink Azalea*' hanging on the wall in a room to his left. He went straight up to it and, sucking his pipe, looked at it silently for some time. Eventually he turned towards me and said, "I have often wondered where that picture went. I congratulate you on having acquired it and, although I say it myself, you have a damned good Cadell," and broke into an infectious laugh."

Bunty developed a close relationship with the Harrison family and often corresponded with Ion Harrison. In a letter of 1st December 1929, he wrote:

"The advantage in buying modern pictures is (1) that the buyer knows the work to be by the artist who paints it; (2) buying comparatively low with the sporting chance, combined with either knowledge or luck, that the picture will go up, and (3) the advantage, and this to the painter – of encouraging contemporary art without which there would be no future 'old masters'!"

He was doubtless referring to Harrison's own collection of contemporary Scottish works and encouraging him to 'continue the good work', especially with regard to his own paintings. Happily, Harrison continued to support Bunty by purchasing paintings on a regular basis, at a time when most people were unable to afford works of art.

For, by 1930 the effect of the worsening general economic conditions were starting to be felt. Bunty reduced the price of his works in an effort to stimulate trade. He cut the price of his 'standard' Iona oils to £20. Similarly, the still life composition '*The Red Fan*', (Plate 45), was sold at the Society of Eight Exhibition in February 1930 for just £35. Financial

Plate 66

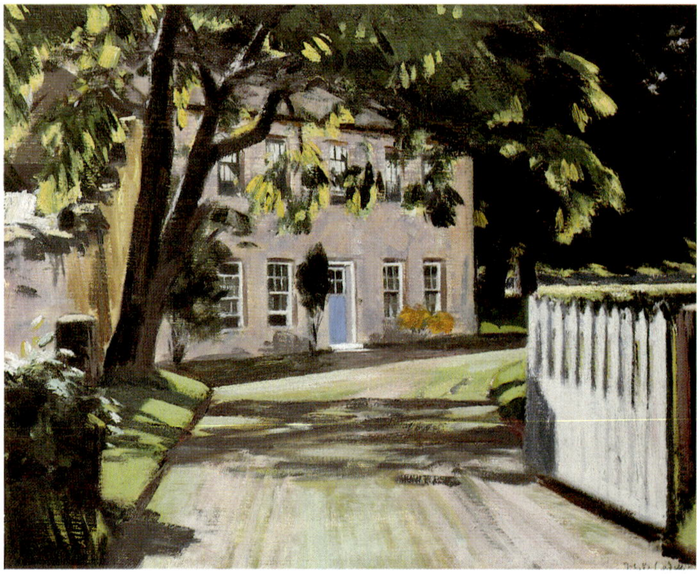

Glenharvie, c. 1930 oil 15 × 18 in.

Plate 67

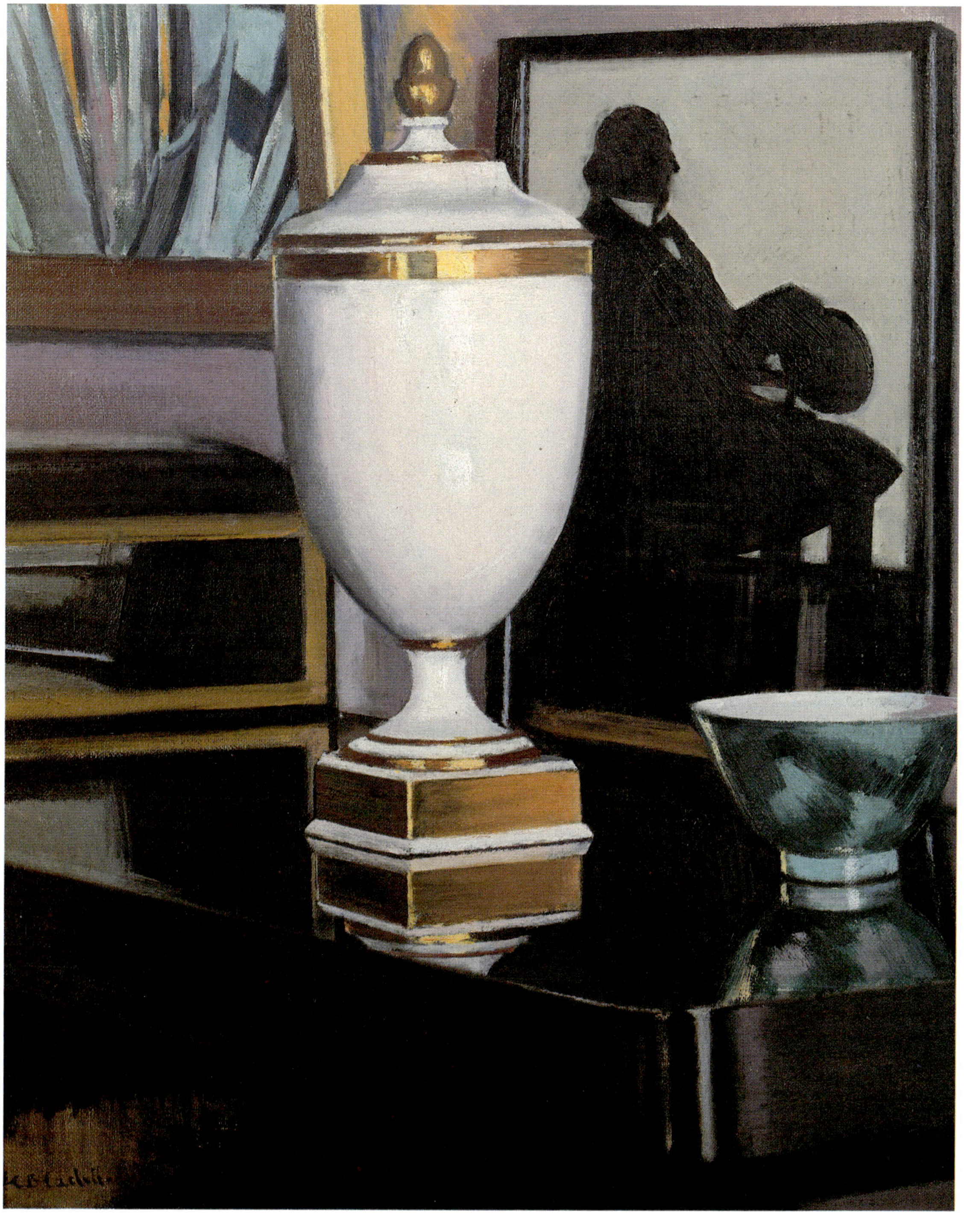

The Wedgwood Vase, 1929 oil 18 × 15 in.

considerations may also have encouraged Bunty to concentrate on (more affordable) water-colours during his stay on Iona between July and September.

By March of the following year, Bunty's relationship with the R.S.A. had improved sufficiently for him to agree to being put forward again for nomination as an Associate. It must have given his old friend James Paterson great pleasure to have sent the letter announcing his election.

ROYAL SCOTTISH ACADEMY

Royal Scottish Academy.

JAMES PATERSON, SECRETARY.
DAVID FOGGIE, TREASURER.
TELEPHONE _ EDINBURGH 27590.

EDINBURGH

19th. March, 1931.

F. C. B. Cadell, Esq., A.R.S.A.
6, Ainslie Place,
Edinburgh.

Dear Sir,

I have the pleasure to inform you that at a General Assembly of the Academy held yesterday afternoon, you were elected to the rank of Associate.

In order to render the election valid, some formalities have to be complied with, and I am asked to enclose an excerpt from the Rules and Regulations relative to the election of Associates.

With reference to Law 43, the signing of the Rules and Obligations in the Book kept by the Secretary will have to be postponed till later in the year. A Committee has just completed the revision of the Laws, and the new edition is now in the hands of the printer. In due course when these have been printed and circulated among the Members, you will be called upon to sign the Rules and the Obligation.

The President and Council offer their cordial congratulations on your election.

Believe me,
Yours faithfully,
James Paterson
Secretary.

It is an appointment that could very well have been made many years earlier had Bunty felt disposed to go back on his rather intransigent view of the importance of the R.S.A. As he himself admitted in a letter to Ion Harrison:

"Lavery wrote to me to convey his congratulations to the R.S.A. who had 'at last seen the light'. But to do the moribund body justice they are not altogether to blame; for in a tantrum of temper I took my name off the waiting list just after the war, and it was only with great persuasion I was induced to put it on again a fortnight before the recent election, so that really is of record speed."

Bunty's election as an A.R.S.A. coincided with a major exhibition in Paris. 'Les Peintres Ecossais' was organised by Duncan MacDonald who had left Aitken Dott in Edinburgh to join A. J. McNeill Reid in Glasgow in 1926, and had then moved to London as part of Alex Reid and Lefevre Ltd. The exhibition was held at Galeries Georges Petit and featured works

Plate 68

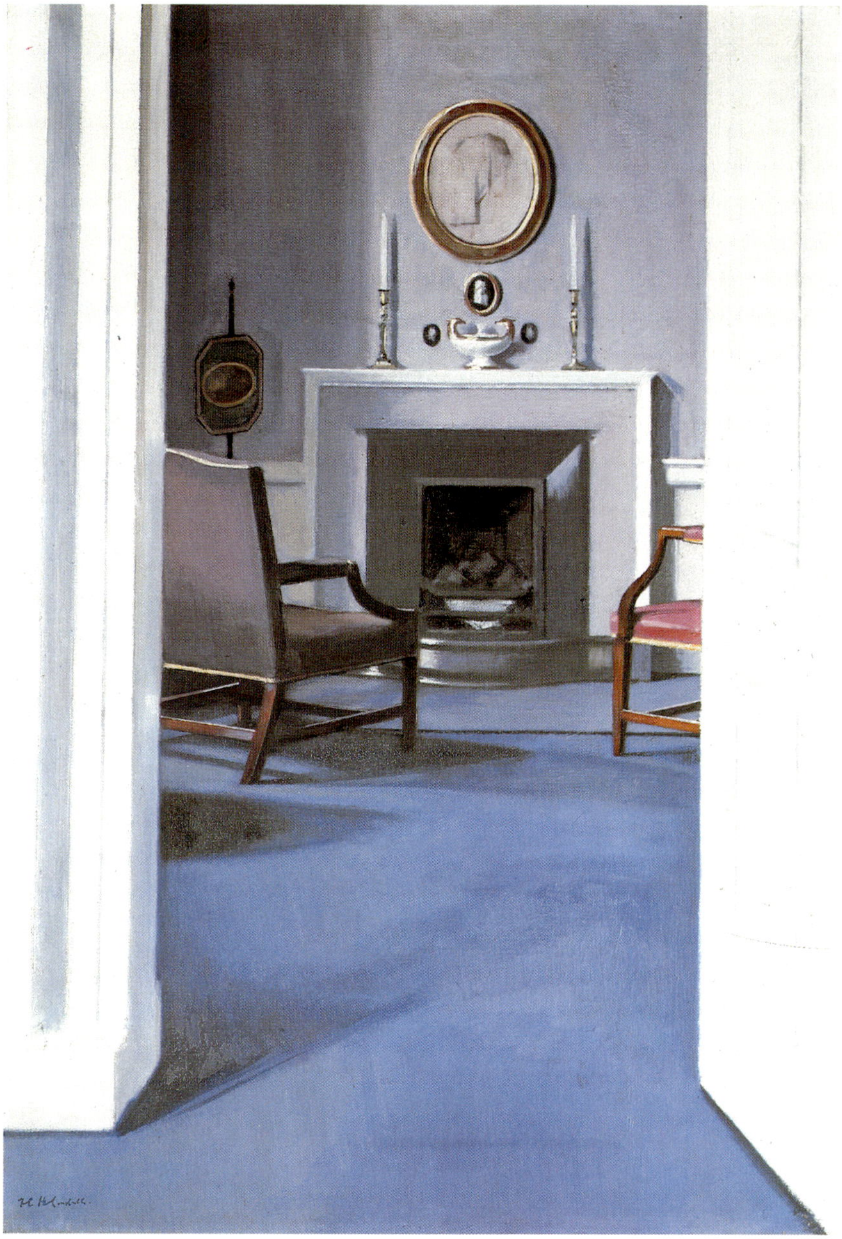

Second Floor, 6 Ainslie Place, c. 1929 oil 30 × 20 in.

by Peploe (10), Fergusson (17), Hunter (7), Cadell (8), Bear (8) and Dunlop (8). It was launched amid great publicity including a letter of support from the British Prime Minister, Ramsay MacDonald. Writing in Apollo, André Salmon described it as:

"One of the very first foreign events of importance organised in one of the oldest Parisian galleries." He went on to comment on Bunty's work, as follows. "Cadell aims also to charm without undesirable concessions. His themes are all full of grace. Yet if he charms, if he wishes to attract people, he imposes tyrannically his taste for rigid line and the kind of geometrical harmony of his most attractive works."

Bunty's preoccupation with 'rigid line' was not something new. Most of his still life works and interiors painted after the war were recognisable by the 'solidity of handling' to which the Observer critic had referred when reviewing the 1923 exhibition at the Leicester Galleries in London. However, the observations that Salmon made do highlight the trend in Bunty's later still life compositions (see Plates 85 & 86) in which he concentrated on creating precise, almost geometric patterns.

By the autumn of 1931, when Bunty returned from Iona, it was clear that the second floor rooms at 6 Ainslie Place were not large enough to accommodate the increasing number of unsold paintings and not prestigious enough to stage an exhibition. Bunty, therefore, took Parson's Galleries on Queen Street for the last three weeks on October. He hung thirty-five watercolours, and fifty-five oils in the four rooms; seven watercolours and five oils were sold.

Plate 69

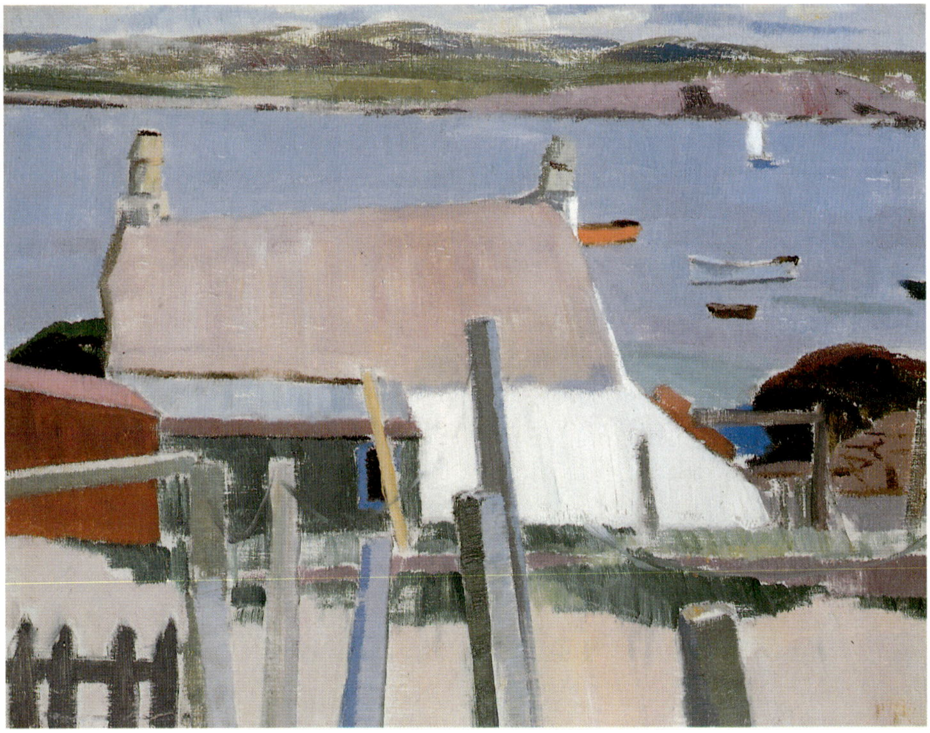

Iona, towards Mull, c. 1932 oil 15 × 18 in.

Plate 70

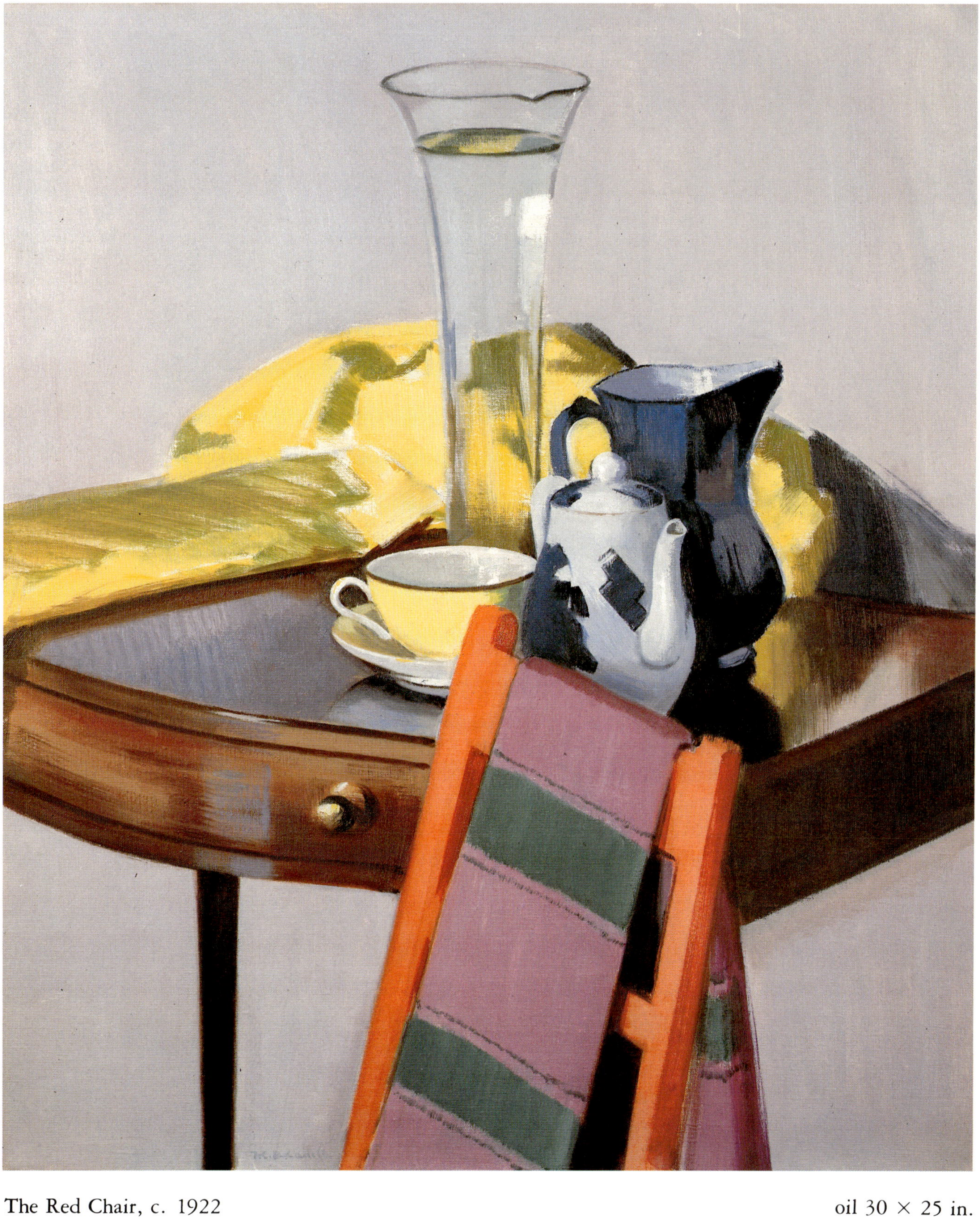

The Red Chair, c. 1922 oil 30 × 25 in.

Plate 71

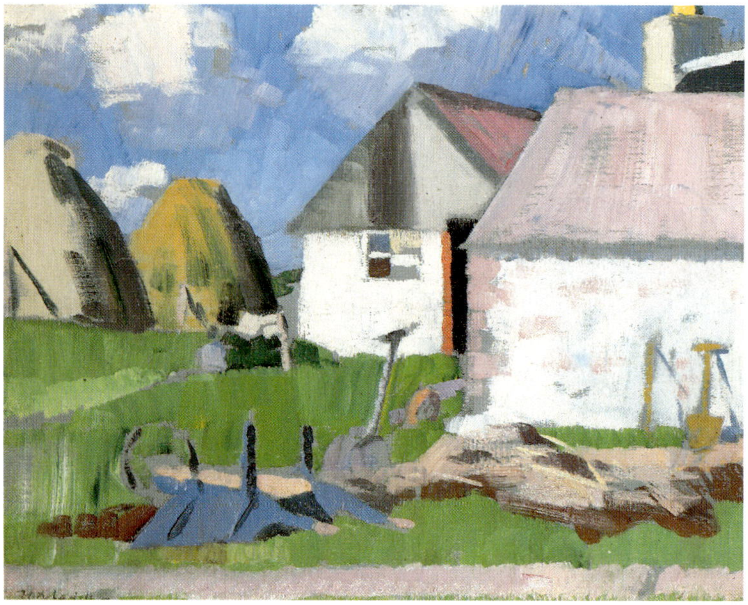

Cottages, Iona, c. 1930 oil 15 × 18 in.

Sadly, this type of response was becoming all too frequent for virtually all artists of the period.

Bunty was left with very little option but to move from the fashionable heart of the 'New Town' district to a less popular part of the city. During the exhibition at Parson's Gallery, he viewed four properties on Regent Terrace that were available for rent and finally settled on No. 30. He did not move there until March 1932, by which time he had agreed to participate in another exhibition organised by Duncan MacDonald. Encouraged by the reviews of the Paris show, MacDonald arranged a show at Barbizon House in London. Apart from the inclusion of paintings by William Gillies, who replaced Dunlop, the artists whose works were shown were the same as at Galleries Georges Petit the year before; (despite Hunter's death in 1931, his work was included).

Bunty did not choose the paintings of his that were shown. Rather like Peploe, who preferred to be absent when 'his' dealers made their choice, Bunty was happy to leave the decision to the organiser of the exhibition. As he explained in a letter to Ion Harrison:

"MacDonald is coming here today or tomorrow to choose pictures of mine for it (the Barbizon House Exhibition). I always prefer this to choosing them myself as salesmen can sell so much better what they like themselves."

MacDonald chose a representative selection of Bunty's work for the show, including some cartoons similar to those that had appeared in the *'Jack and Tommy'* book. 'The Studio' critic referred to these as "amusing and skilful sketches of war-time types" and goes on to praise Bunty for his broad handling of clean prismatic colour.

Apart from a Royal Academy Exhibition of Scottish Art in 1934, the Barbizon House Exhibition was the last one of Bunty's work in the capital until after his death.

Plate 72

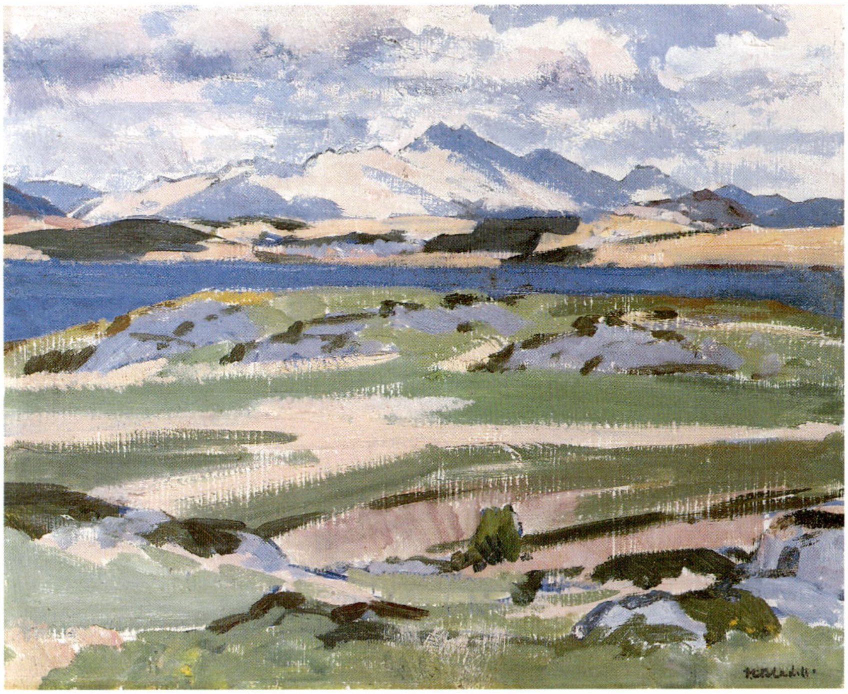

Ben Cruachan, 1930 oil 15 × 18 in.

Plate 73

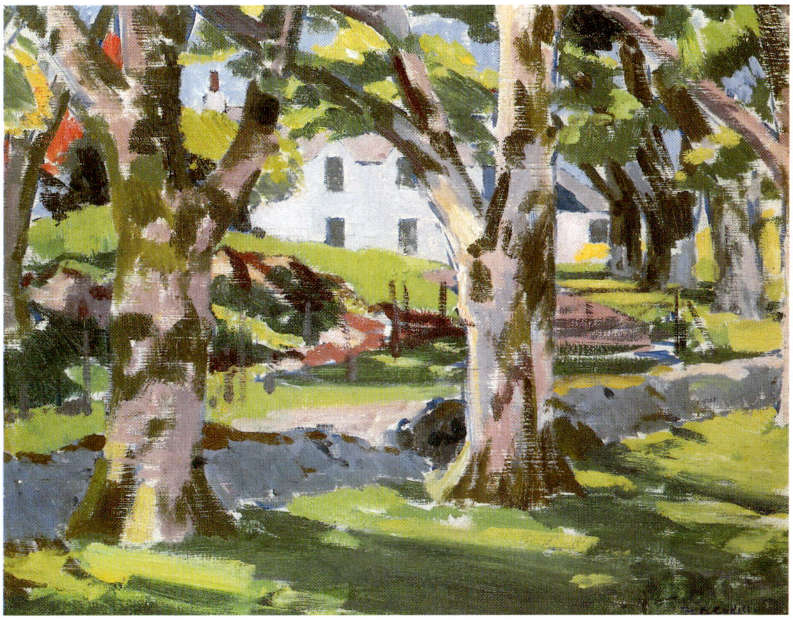

Auchnacraig, c. 1931 oil 15 × 18 in.

Plate 74

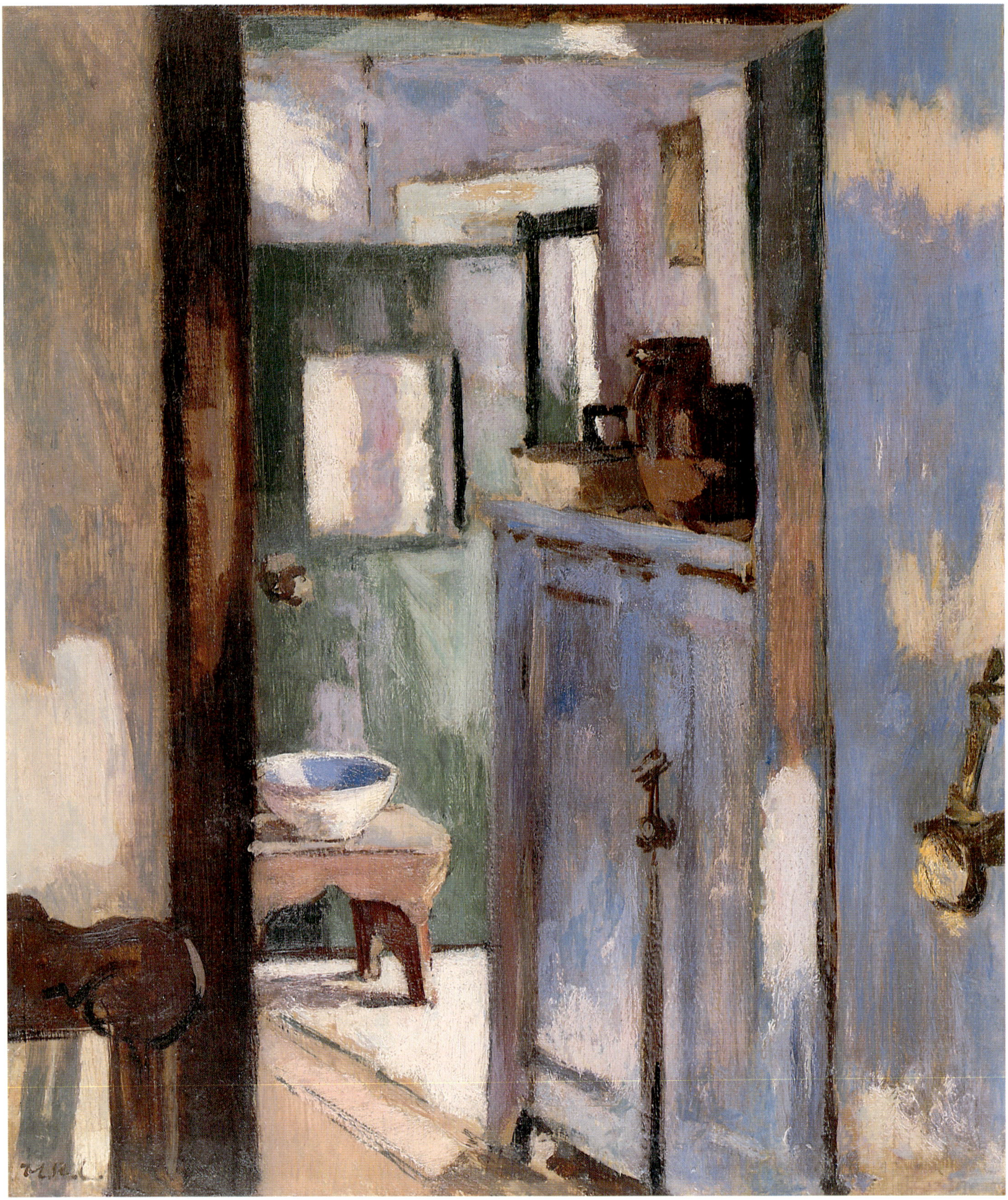

Inside Iona Croft, c. 1930 oil 18 × 15 in.

Chapter Six

1932–1937

Although the new studio at 30 Regent Terrace was not in such a fashionable part of Edinburgh as 6 Ainslie Place, it did have compensating features. One was the extra space that it provided (including a large sunken bath), while another was the magnificent view over Holyrood House towards Arthur's Seat which Bunty captured in *'The Open Window'* (Plate 93). He described his new home as being 'a perfect prospect for a town house'. While the outlook was stunning, the proximity to some of the city's less savoury elements meant that it was not long before Bunty was attacked by a local ruffian while walking home one evening. The injuries he suffered seemed superficial at the time, but their effects resurfaced a few years later to complicate his treatment for a painful sinus condition that was finally diagnosed as cancer.

The west coast of Scotland was blessed with beautiful weather during the early summer of 1932 and by the beginning of June Bunty was back on Iona. Peploe, who had become almost as regular a visitor to the island as Bunty, had not arrived by the end of the month. Bunty wrote to him on 7th July.

"How are you? It must have been rather awful in a way in Edinburgh all June if the weather there was as fine as it was here. But you didn't really lose much from the painting point of view. Little colour, not much wind and a cloudless sky for the most part. Though lying about doing nothing but benefitting the health was very pleasant. I have painted a few watercolours, four or five oil panels and a 24 inch square of the Nunnery; this is not yet finished as I have only done about ¾ of the stones! The panels consist of . . . and a portrait of myself done in a disused mirror and not yet completed. Anything to escape the horrors of Ben More . . .!"

This extract from a much longer letter helps to emphasize the special characteristics of Iona that appealed to so many artists of the period, and to Bunty in particular. Prolonged periods of fine weather destroyed the very challenge on which Bunty thrived – to try and capture the sudden and dramatic changes in light, and therefore colour, of the island's natural subject matter which 'normal' weather conditions brought. The sea could change from a dull grey to a brilliant aquamarine in seconds. The colour of the dark rocks and contrasting white sand, of the brown sea-weed and the green machair turf, changed more subtly. But it was Bunty's ability to retain these marvellous colours and tones for long enough to commit them to canvas, panel or paper that was the key to his most successful Iona paintings.

In contrast, it was total anathema to Bunty to paint what he considered to be hackneyed and mundane subjects, of which the rather plain view of Ben More was a perfect example. The *'Self-portrait'* (Plate 76) is probably the 'strongest' one that he painted. The rather severe treatment of his own features is in contrast to the much more sympathetic handling of *'Able Seaman Vickery'* (Plate 75), executed at about the same time.

Among the many visitors to Iona during the summer of 1932, was John Perceval Clark, (Jean's only son, who changed his surname to Cadell on his father's death in 1936). John was

Plate 75

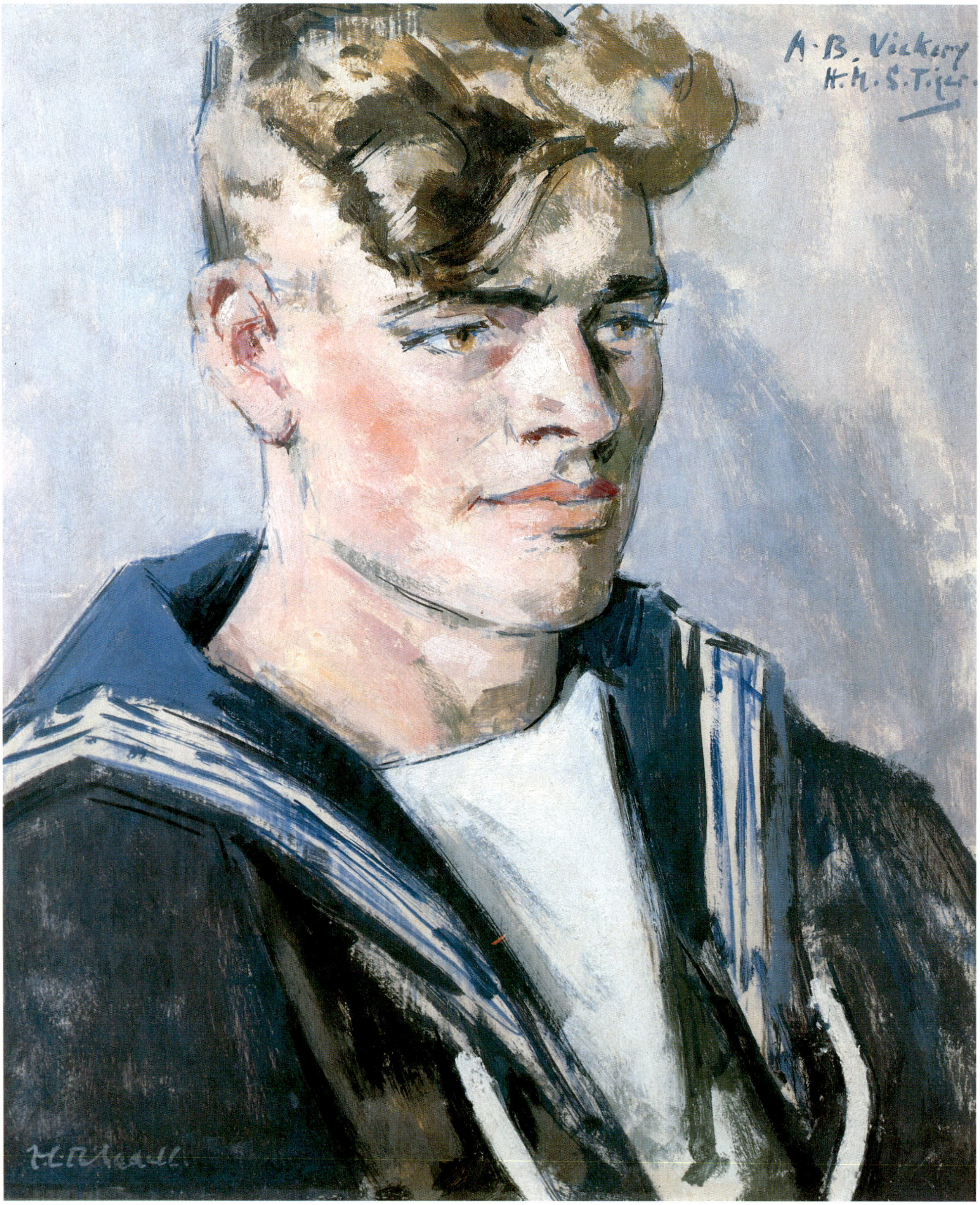

Able Seaman Vickery, c. 1932 oil 18 × 15 in.

Plate 76

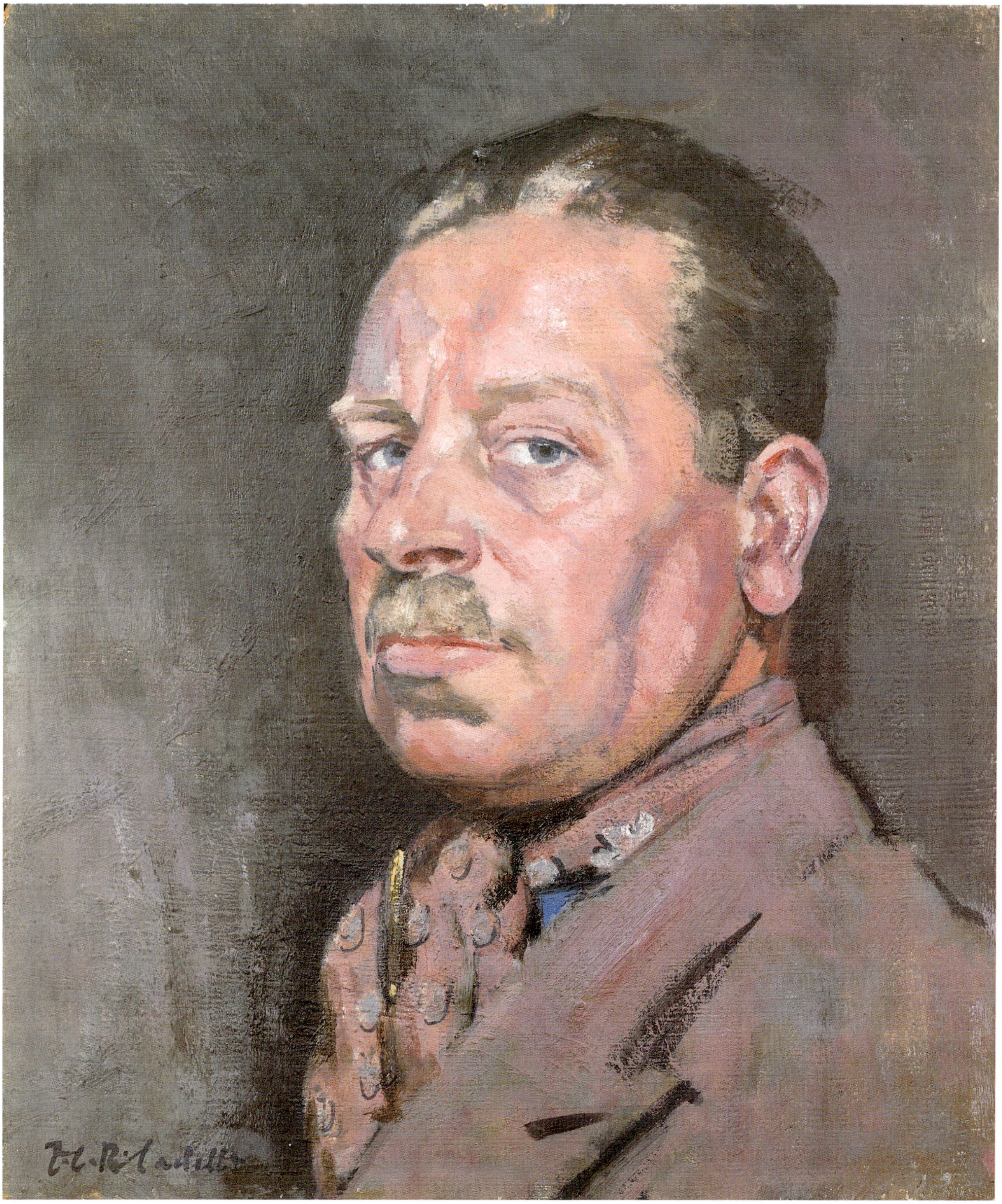

Self-portrait, 1932 oil 18 × 15 in.

Plate 77

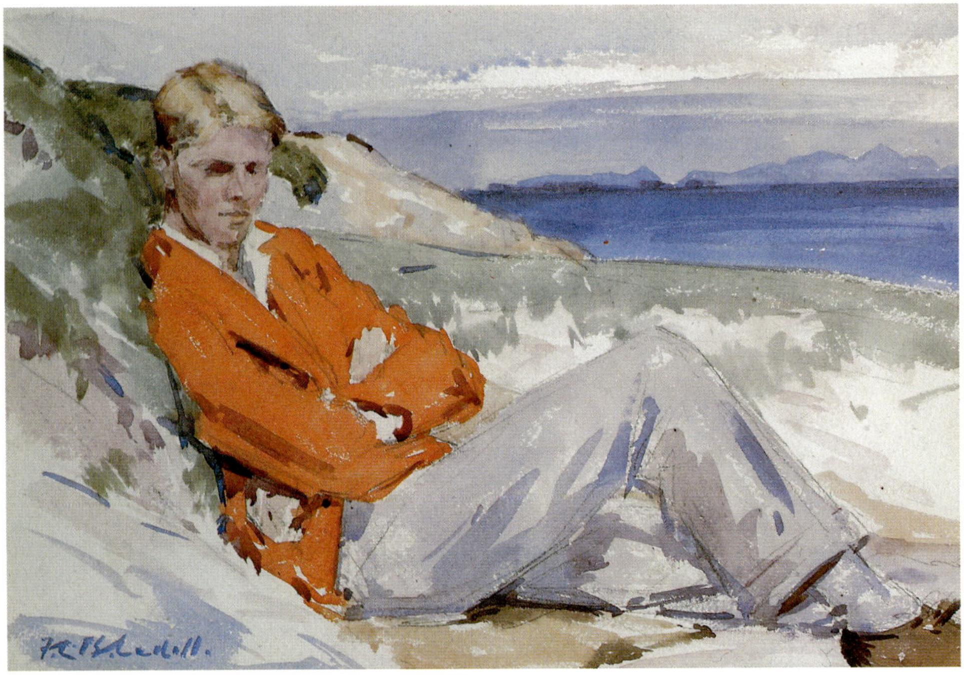

John Cadell, 1932 watercolour 11 × 16 in.

then a pupil at Loretto and sported the school's well known red blazer – perfect subject matter for Bunty. The watercolour of John in a school uniform (Plate 77) was exhibited in October that year at Bunty's one man show at The Scottish Gallery. It was a measure of the times that only one of sixty-one paintings at the exhibition sold, two were given away as wedding presents and fourteen were consigned to Pearson and Westergaard who, by then, had taken over as Bunty's main dealer in Glasgow.

It was probably on his return from Iona in 1932 that Bunty stayed with the Harrisons in Helensburgh, and painted the *'Interior, Croft House'* (Plate 78). It was first shown at The Society of Eight's twenty-first exhibition in January 1933, and is one example of Bunty's finest work. The viewer's eye is almost magnetically drawn through the open door across the polished floor to the focal point of the painting – the brilliant red seat-cover. On the way, one passes a 'natural' still life composition of irises on the table on the left, balanced by a Peploe still life of roses and fruit on the wall above the sideboard on the right of the door. Similarly, the Cadell still life above the sideboard on the right of the chair in the dining room is cleverly offset by the pattern on the curtain to its left. But not only is the painting so subtly balanced in composition and perspective, but in colour too. A myriad of different colours and tones is used, but in total harmony. It is difficult to imagine a painting that contains so much subject matter remaining uncluttered.

Painted in 1933, the portrait of Mrs. Harrison (Plate 79), seems rather cramped and contrived by comparison. The painting does not have the same inspirational feel to it as the Croft House Interior. It was, perhaps, partly that Bunty did not really enjoy portrait painting and partly a reflection of his state of mind in that the economic realities of life were

Plate 78

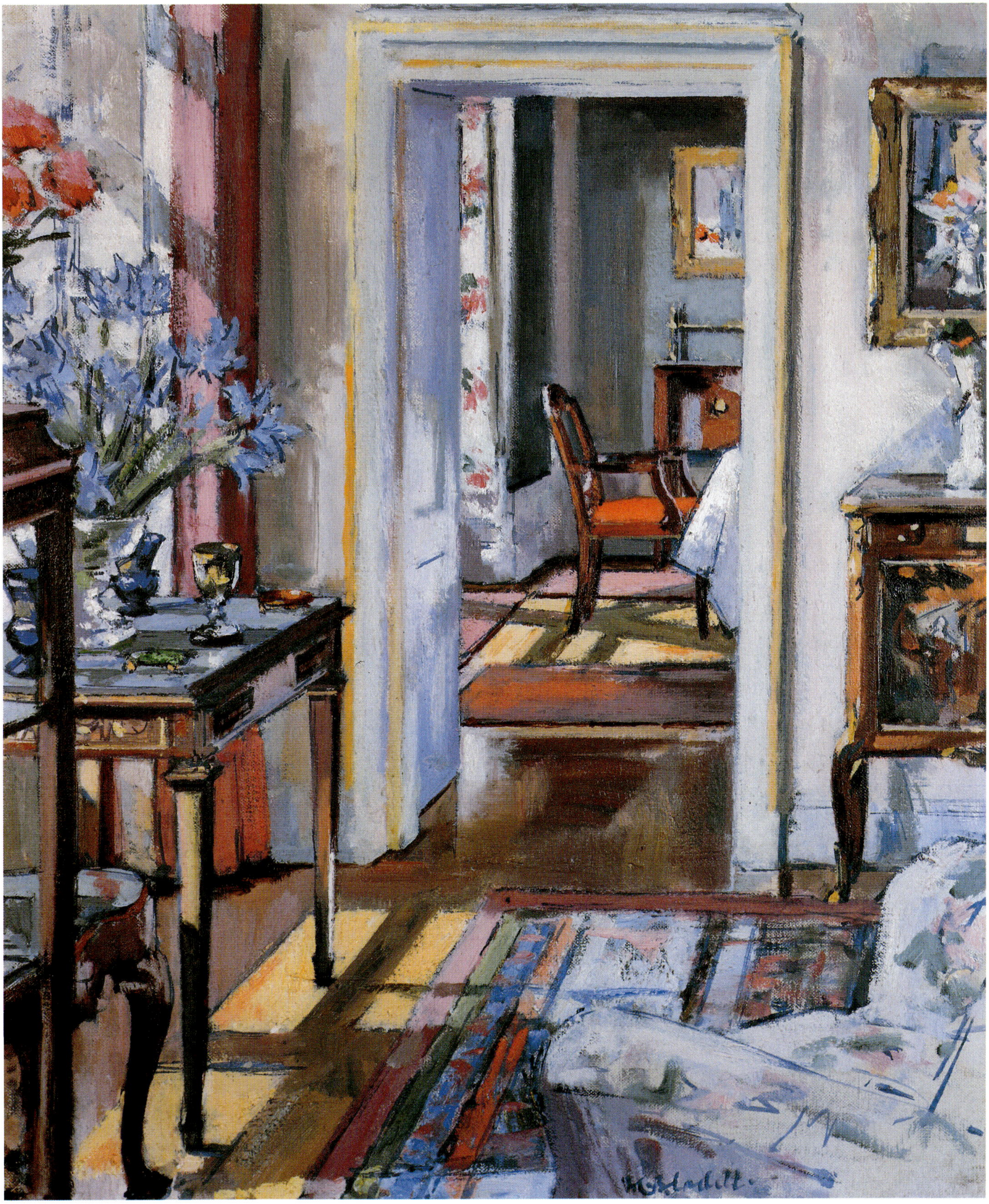

Interior, Croft House, 1932

oil 24 × 20 in.

Plate 79

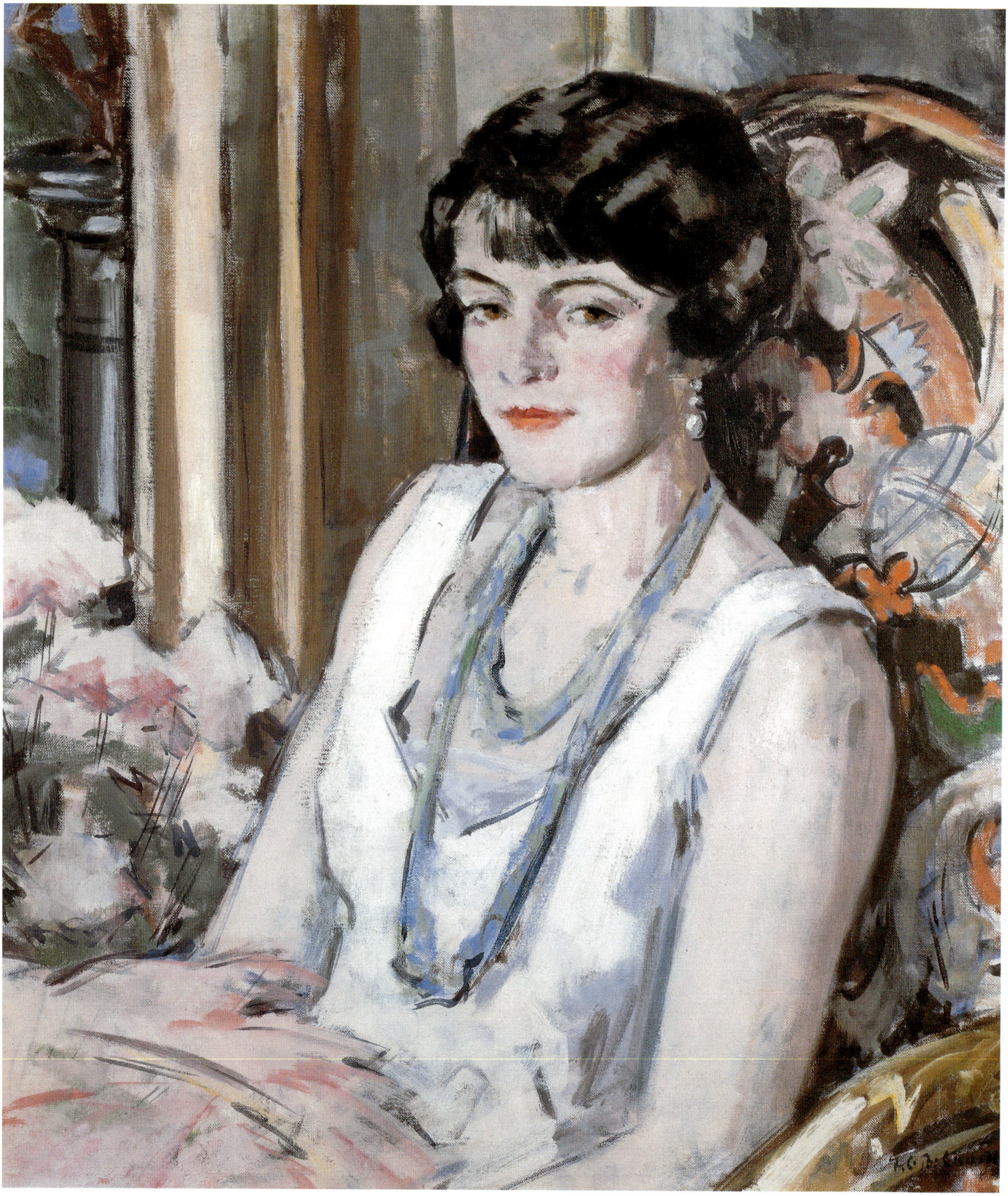

Mrs Harrison 1933

oil 24 × 20 in.

clearly nothing but depressing. Outwardly, however, Bunty remained his ebullient self, making light of his own difficulties. In a letter to Harrison he wrote:

"Things are hellish, and if one fine day you see me sitting at Maule's corner with an upturned Lincoln Bennet don't be too surprised to drop a penny in it. Such is life! Who wants a future one – what an inducement to Christianity – a man on a thing that sounds like a fog-horn is blowing 'Hark the Herald Angels' outside the house as I write – Blast him!"

He held an exhibition of watercolours and drawings at 30 Regent Terrace just before Christmas which was supported mainly by his friends. Fifteen works sold for £78. With this level of public response, it was hardly surprising that the major dealers were not keen to go to the expense of holding large exhibitions; and although Pearson and Westergaard held one man shows for Bunty in both 1933 and 1934 in Glasgow, they were the last to be put on during his life.

Plate 80

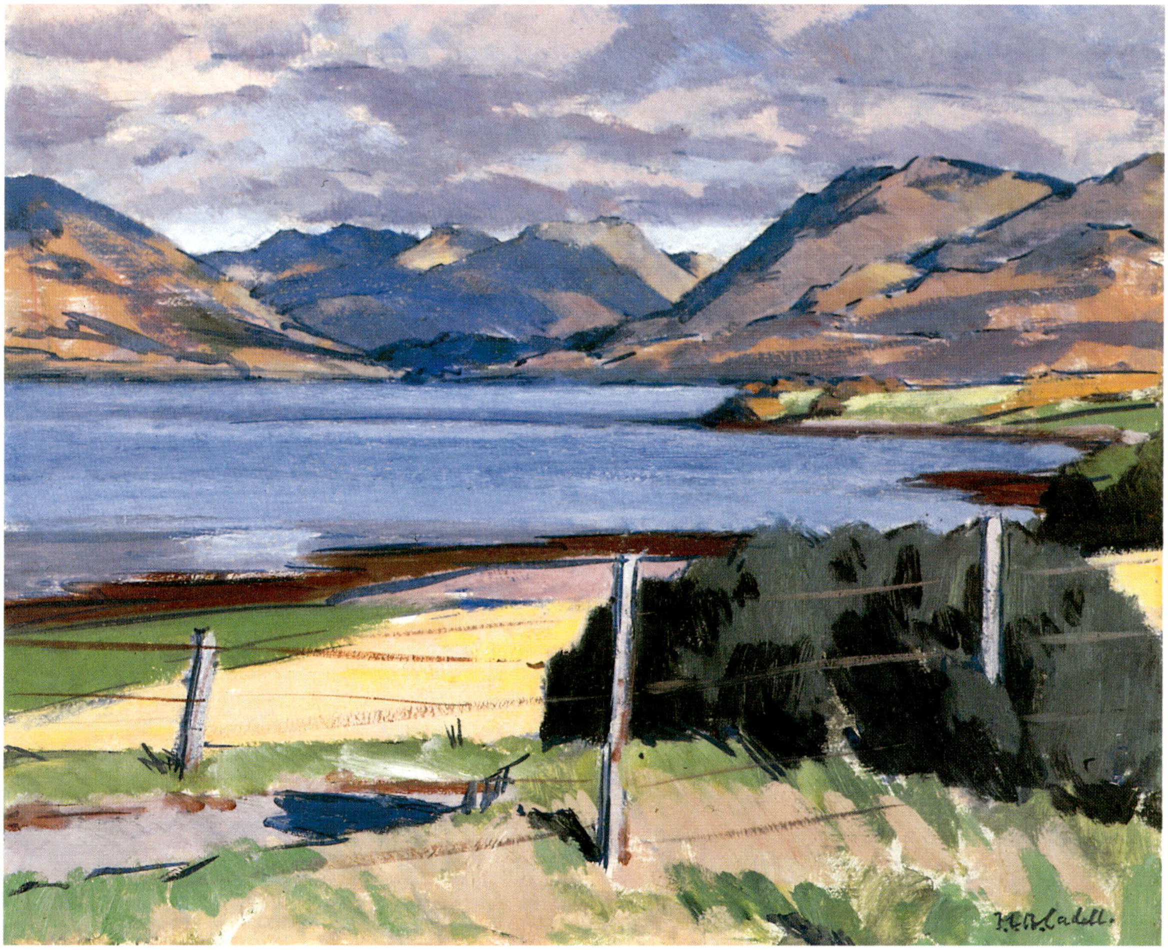

Loch Creran, Argyll, c. 1928 oil 15 × 18 in.

It was during 1934 that Bunty's health started to show signs of deterioration. Having never been fond of tramcars, and having spoken strongly against their introduction to the centre of Edinburgh in 1922, it was somewhat ironic that the first of his accidents should involve one. His report of the incident to Ion Harrison again demonstrates Bunty's ability to maintain his sense of humour in the face of obvious discomfort.

"I fell down the stairs of one of our infernal tramcars and landed on the tail of my spine on one of their metal-edged steps. Since when I have been unable to do anything but stand up. I have also developed deafness in my right ear – temporary I hope – though it may be the beginning of the end!"

Undaunted by this and other painful accidents he continued to paint despite the accumulation of work in his studio. By now, on much better terms with the R.S.A., he was determined to put forward at least some new works for inclusion in the six spaces allotted to him, as an Associate, in the annual exhibition. He also ensured that he was well represented at the R.G.I. and at the Society of Eight.

It was during the 1935 Society of Eight Exhibition in January that Bunty learned of his election as a member of the Royal Scottish Society of Painters in Watercolour (R.S.W.). He was the only one of the four Scottish Colourists to be a member of both the R.S.A. and R.S.W. It was one of the few pieces of good news that the year was to bring. By the spring, economic considerations had made it necessary to move house yet again, this time to 4 Warriston Crescent, on the northern edge of the 'New Town'. But probably the most

Plate 81

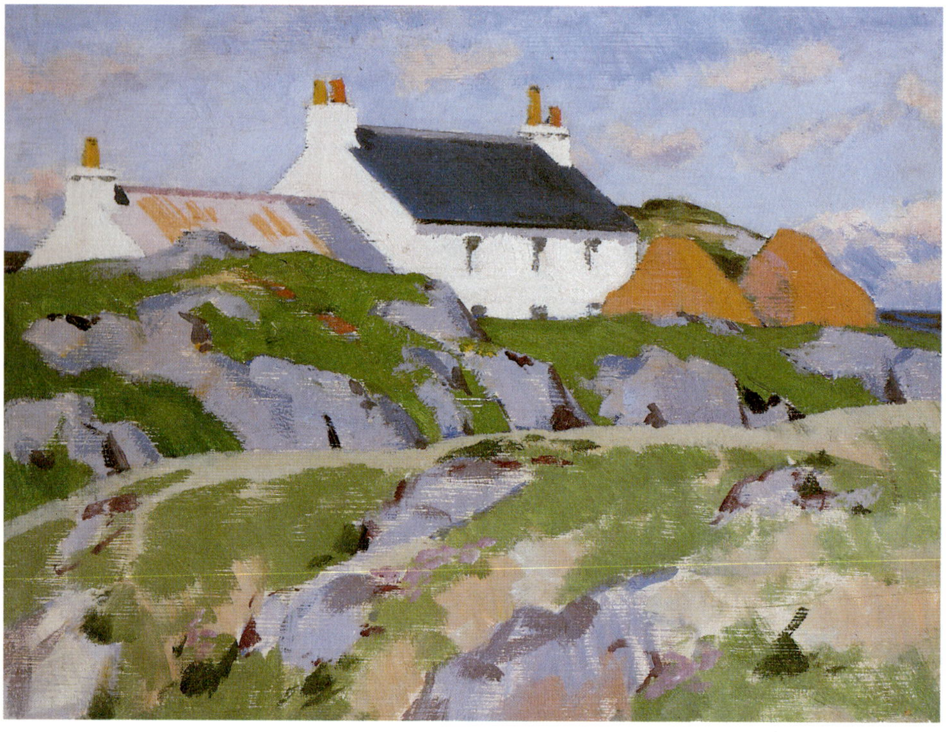

Iona Croft, c. 1933 oil 15 × 18 in.

Plate 82

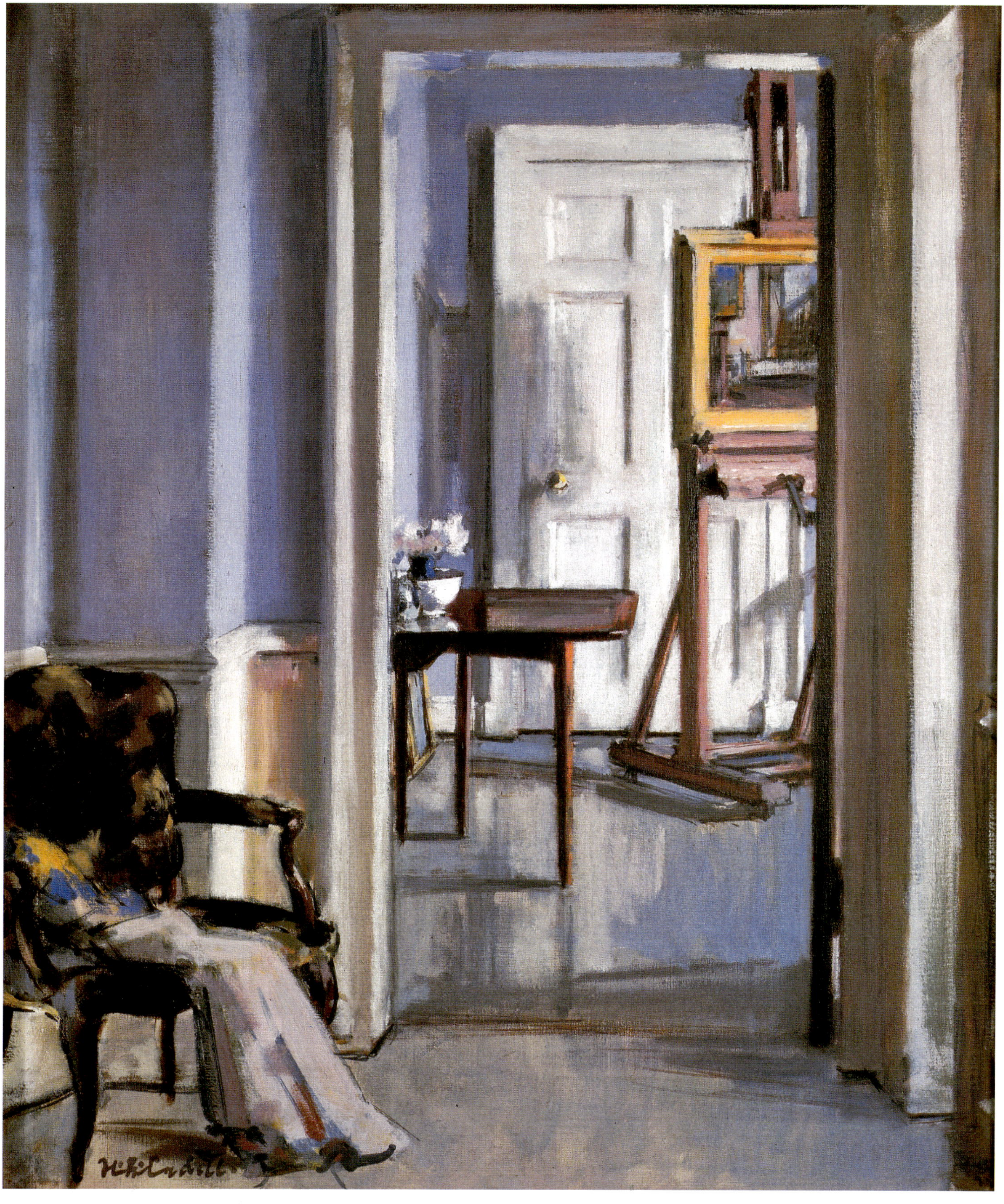

30 Regent Terrace, c. 1934 oil 24 × 20 in.

devastating blow that Bunty suffered was the news of Peploe's death in October. He attended the funeral in the company of Ion Harrison, who later wrote:

"Cadell was frightfully nervous and very upset at the loss of his close friend. It was almost as if he had a foreboding that he himself had not long to live. At the graveside, Cadell was so distressed that he had to walk away from the mourners. He just could not bear it."

By the end of 1935, Bunty himself was not well, though his characteristic good humour showed no sign of deserting him. With the death of Peploe and the resignation of John Duncan, the Society of Eight was something of a misnomer; Bunty did his best to fill the vacant spaces and to clear out his own studio by entering fifty-seven works for the annual exhibition in January 1936. There was a complete cross-section of his work including '*Self-portrait*' 1914, (Plate 30). It was a wrench to have to consider selling it, and the quoted price of £150 made almost certain that it would still be there by the end of the show.

Later in the year, Bunty was elected a Royal Scottish Academician. The photograph on page 90 of him together with J. M. Aiken and D. M. Sutherland, just after their election gives no hint of his illness; rather, it shows a glint in his eyes and the beginning of a smile on his lips.

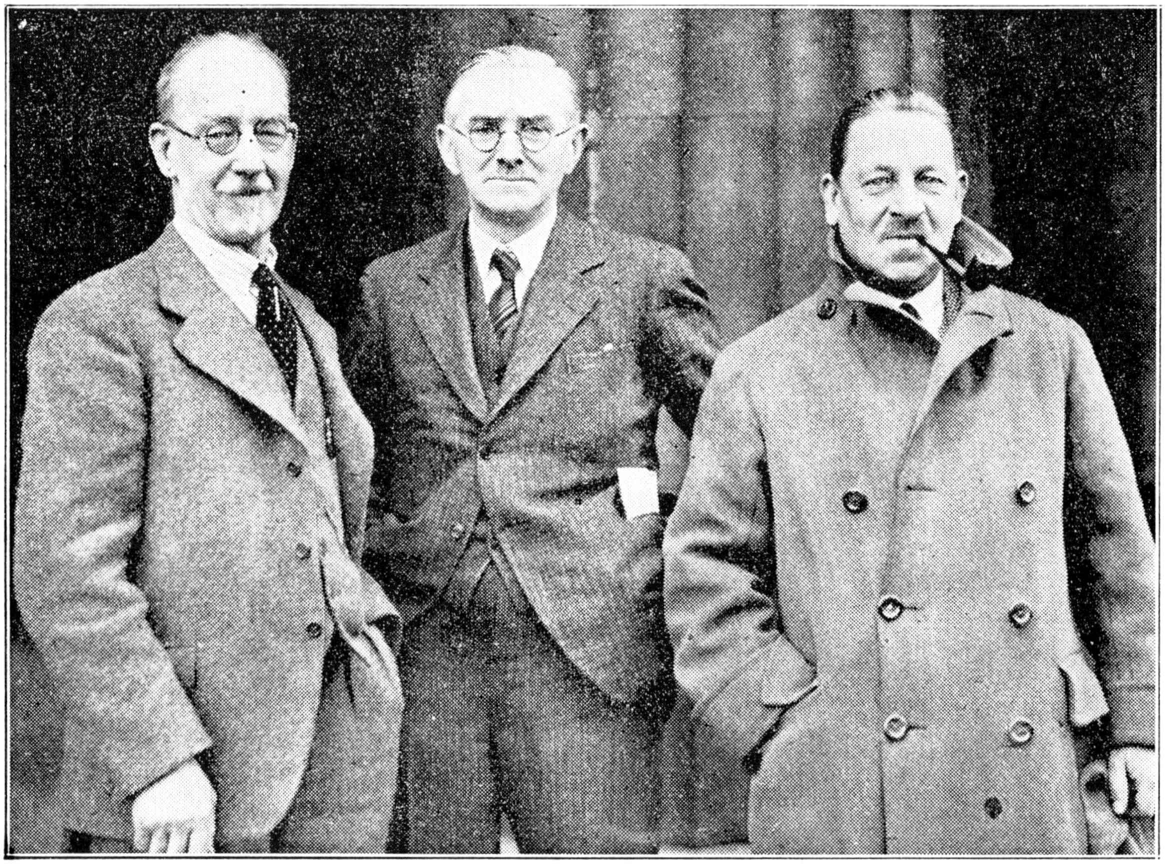

Behind the appearance, the reality was quite different. In August 1936, Bunty made an application to 'The Alexander Nasmyth Fund for the Relief of Decayed Scottish Artists'.

He sent more paintings to auction, and Dowell's sold six oils at the end of October for just over £51. By December, Bunty's health had deteriorated further but his wit remained as sharp as ever. Before Christmas, he attended the premiere of Sir James Barrie's Play 'The Boy

APPLICANT'S DECLARATION.

1. Are you of Scottish birth; if not, how long have you been domiciled in Scotland?	1. Yes.
State whether you are a professional Artist; and if so, in what branch you have practised	Yes - Painting.
2. When and where have your works been exhibited? . . .	2. Edinburgh - Glasgow - London Paris. etc. etc.
3. Have you any relatives in a position to assist you? . . .	3. No.
4. Are you a beneficiary of any Annuity fund, or do you derive an income from any other source than your profession? . . . . State amount of your income from every source, including temporary assistance given by relatives or friends	4. No other source of income than professional earnings which I put at an average of about £280. to £300.
5. What is your age?	5. 53.
6. Are you married, widowed, or single?	6. Single.
7. Have you any children living; if so, state how many, giving age and sex of each?	7. No.
8. How are they employed?	8. —
9. To what cause or causes do you attribute your present difficulties?	9. Failure of purchasers - death of Patrons, & difficulties in connection with my house in Ainslie Place - since disposed of.

I do hereby declare that all the questions contained in this paper are herein fully and truly answered to the best of my knowledge and belief.*

Dated this Twentysixth day of August 1936.

Signed, F. C. B. Cadell.

Residence, 4 Warriston Crescent - Edinburgh.

N.B.—Christian and Surname, with Address, to be written at full length.

Francis - Campbell - Boileau - Cadell.

* **Any wilful deception, prevarication, or concealment in this declaration, or in the attestations appended, will cause an applicant to be excluded from the benefits of the Alexander Nasmyth Fund.**

David' with Sir Patrick Ford. On seeing the Philistines stripped to the waist appear on the stage, Ford asked Bunty: "What's the big idea – this half-naked army?" The reply was immediate, "They've put their shirts on David".

By February 1937, Bunty was forced to go into hospital in Edinburgh. He wrote to his sister from the Officers Association Nursing Home in Belgrave Crescent.

"Just a line – for I am feeling very tired – to thank you for your letter and the £5. Dr. Flett who was here this a.m. says that after all I have been through, this condition will go on for 2 or 3 months . . . he thinks I should stay longer and not leave here until I feel that the time has arrived when I myself feel ready to do battle . . ."

Despite the surgery that he was forced to undergo for a cancerous growth in his head, Bunty insisted on continuing his life as normally as possible. Three works were entered for the R.S.A. annual exhibition, including *'The Blue Room'*, (Plate 84). This powerful view of Ainslie Place had originally been purchased by George Service in 1926, but was later

Plate 83

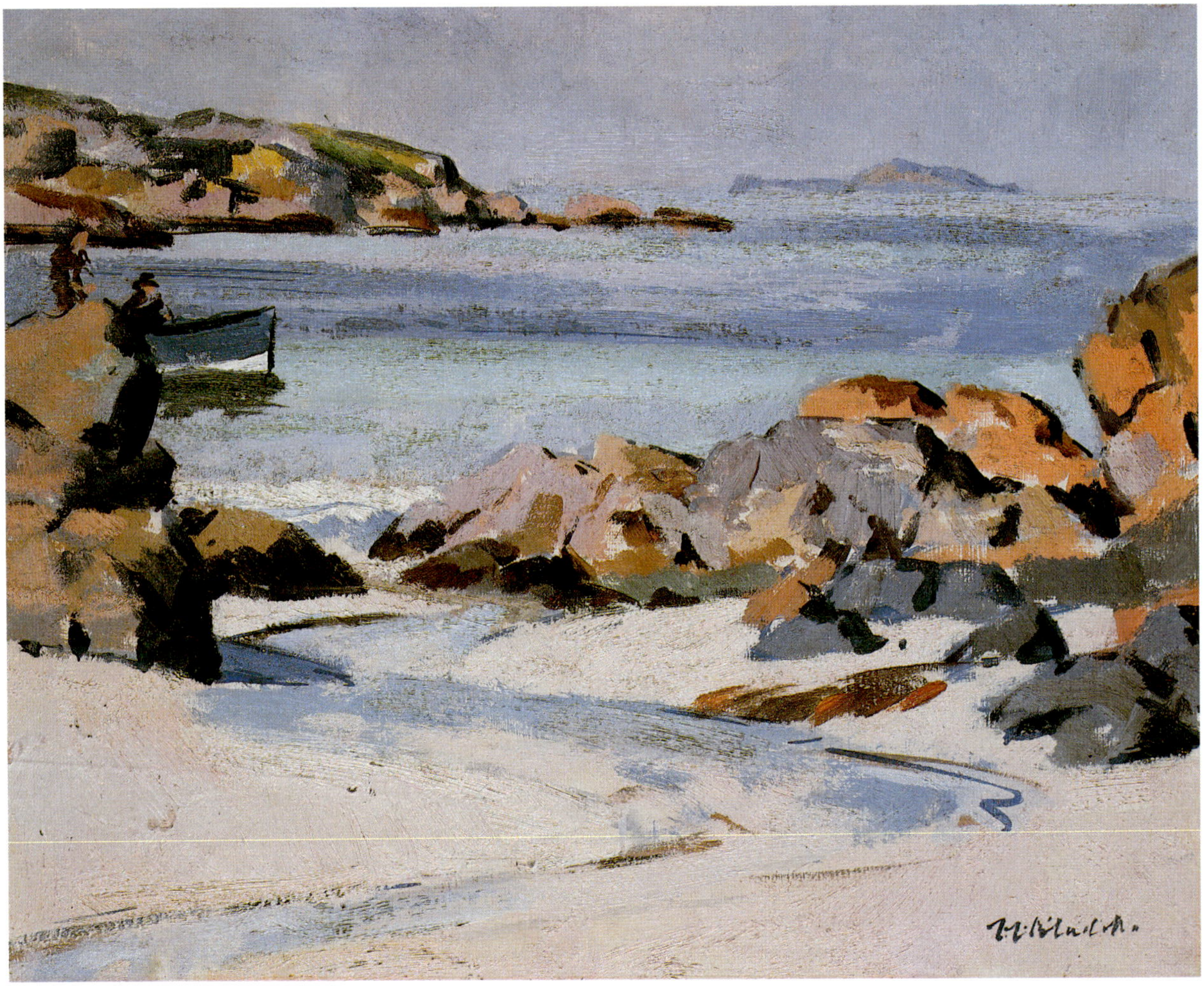

Offshore Iona, c. 1933 oil 15 × 18 in.

Plate 84

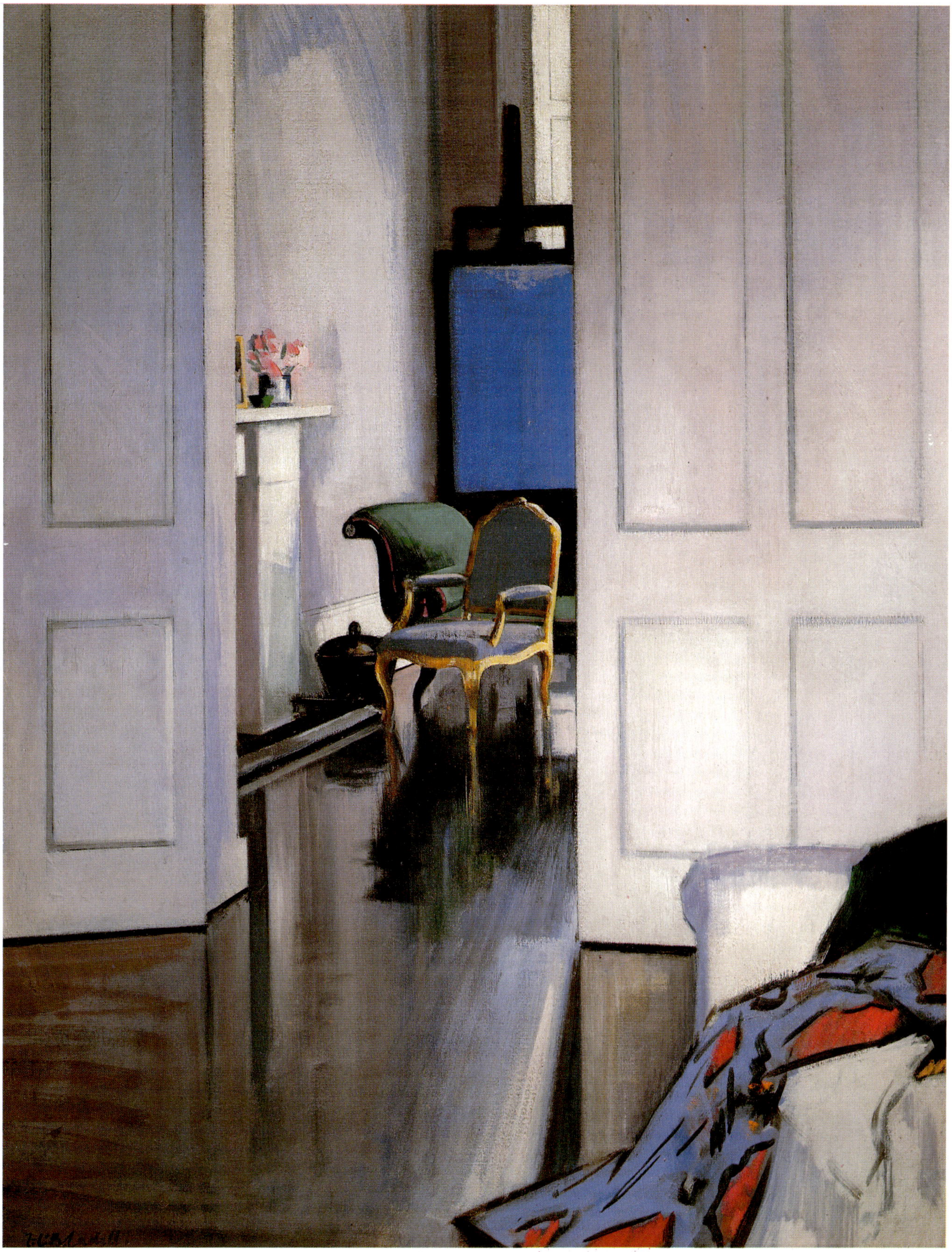

The Blue Room, 1926 oil 40 × 30 in.

Plate 85

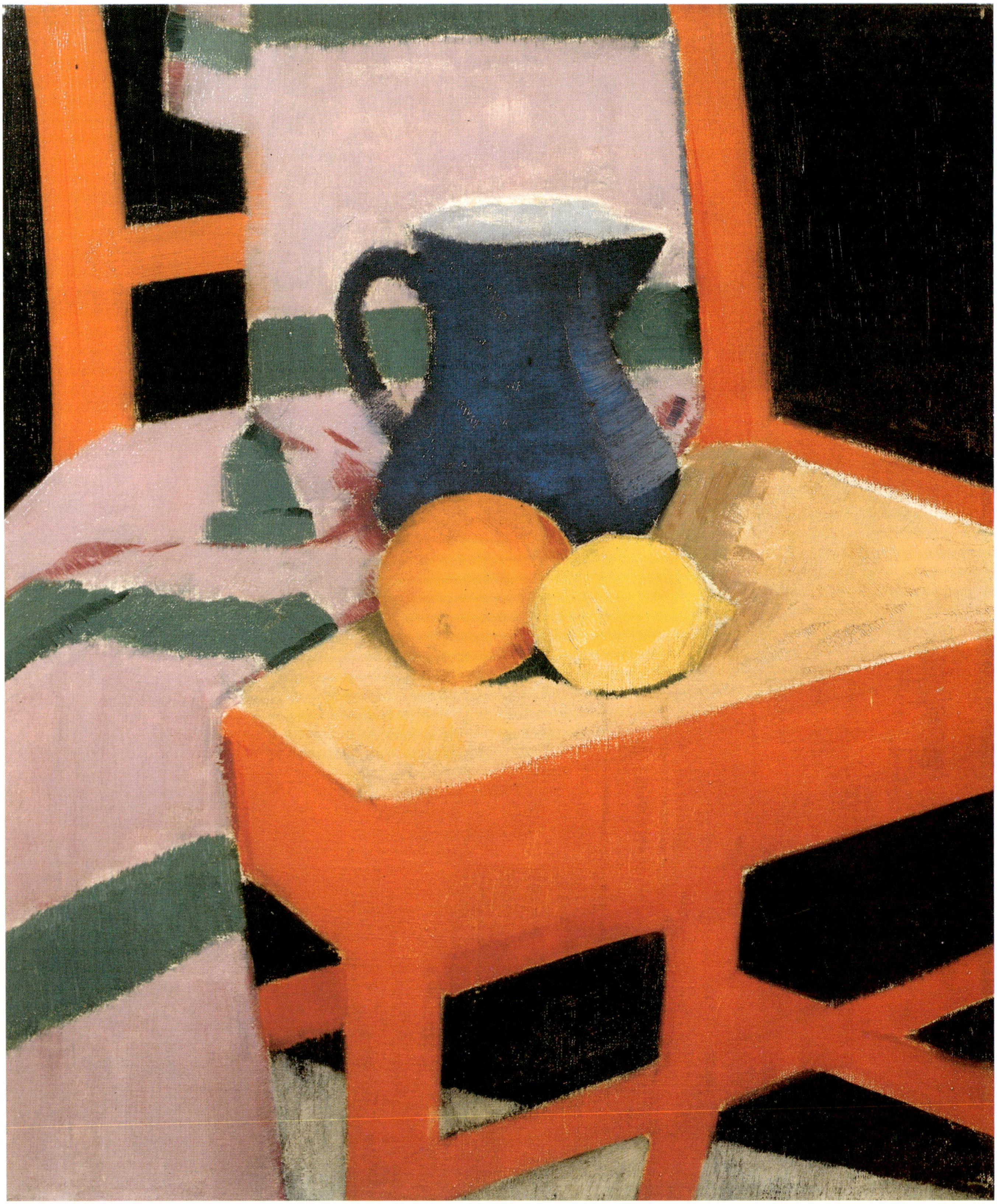

The Red Chair, c. 1922 oil 24 × 20 in.

Plate 86

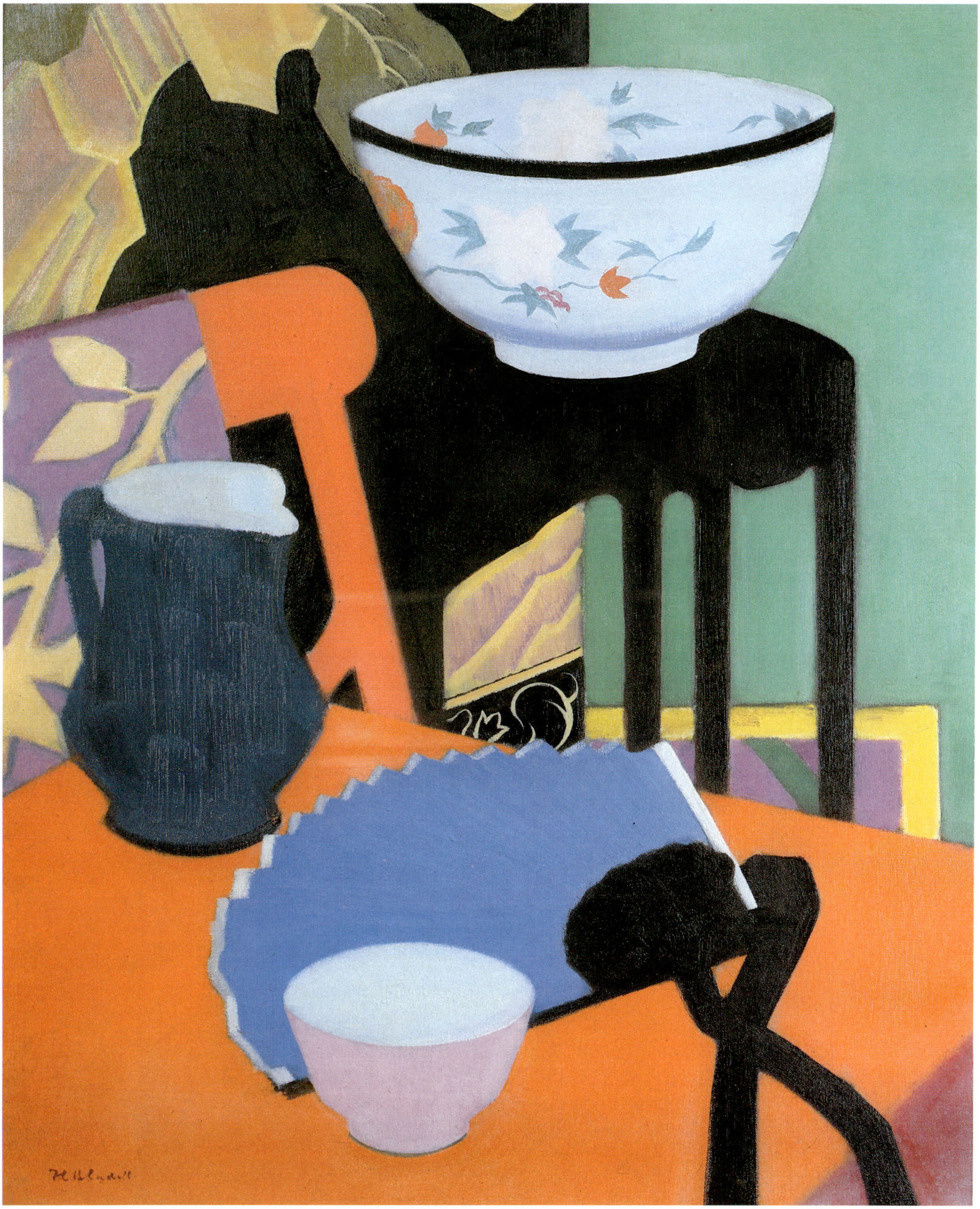

The Blue Fan, c. 1922 oil 24 × 20 in.

exchanged for other paintings. It is probable that it was the painting to which his friend J. J. Cowan referred when writing to Bunty in the late 1920's.

"John Duncan was with me at lunch yesterday and agreed with me that the open door between your studio and the approach thereto is one of the very best of your pictures."

The paintings were the last ones exhibited at the R.S.A. during his lifetime for, by the end of September, Bunty was back in hospital. He wrote again from the nursing home on 9th October.

"I have been here now a fortnight today but simply could not write – the very thought of it tired me. Jaundice is what I have and something wrong with my inside – very swollen and uncomfortable. They seem to think it will answer to treatment – if not a slight operation will have to be performed . . . I sailed through some of the most lovely parts of Scotland the other day in superb weather but took no more interest in it all than I would have in Queen Victoria Station . . . I sleep well despite the hour (6.30 a.m.) at which this is written as I get to sleep usually about 8.30 p.m."

A month later Bunty was still in hospital. He wrote on 10th November:

Plate 87

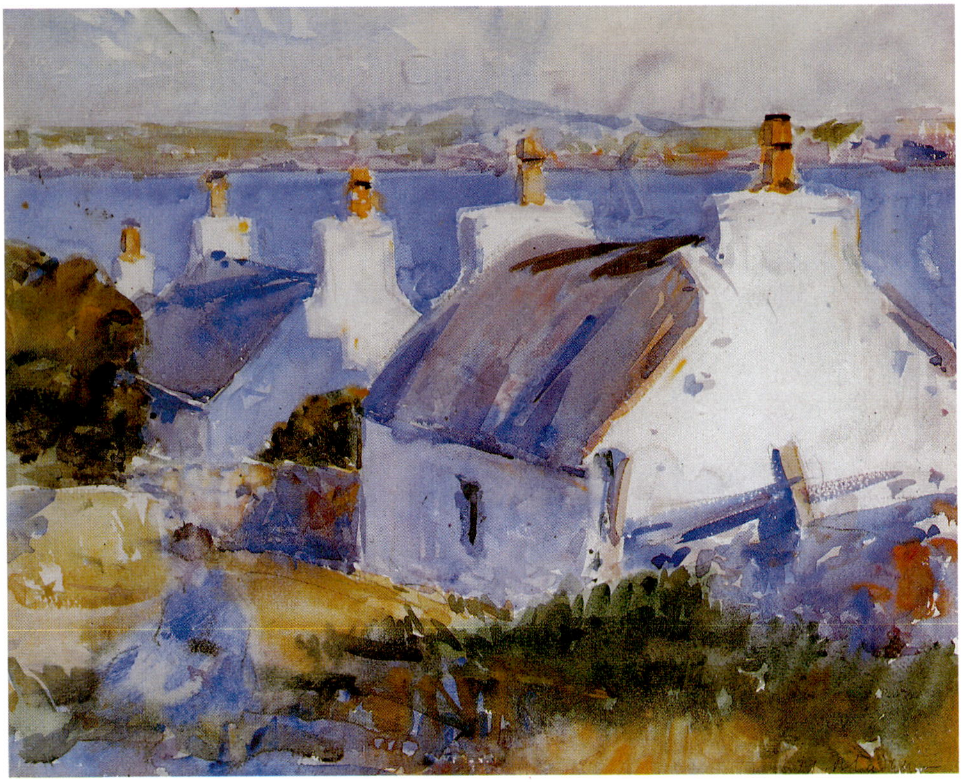

An Iona Croft, 1935 watercolour 15 × 18 in.

"It is now over six weeks since I have been in bed – I don't know what they are going to do with me. They have 'tapped' the tummy once but the accumulation of liquid is worse than ever and my girth is monstrous! The growth in my head is also returning and it is only nine months since I had all that awful business before. I can eat hardly anything though I am not dieted in any way. Thank goodness a bad cough I have had for a week and which kept me from sleeping has gone. Now you know all about me! A depressing rigmarole."

It is one of the last letters that Bunty wrote. He died of cancer on 6th December. There were many tributes, but none more apposite than Sir Patrick Ford's:

"The bright light is quenched now: the wit and laughter
Are silent: the fearless, free spirit at rest,
That flinched not from pain, and that laughed at disaster.
What of gloom is and mourning, are ours that are left.

With line that was flawless and brilliance of colour
His art ran the gamut of beauty in things –
From mirth through to sadness, but never to dullness –
Then take heart and be fearless, remembering him."

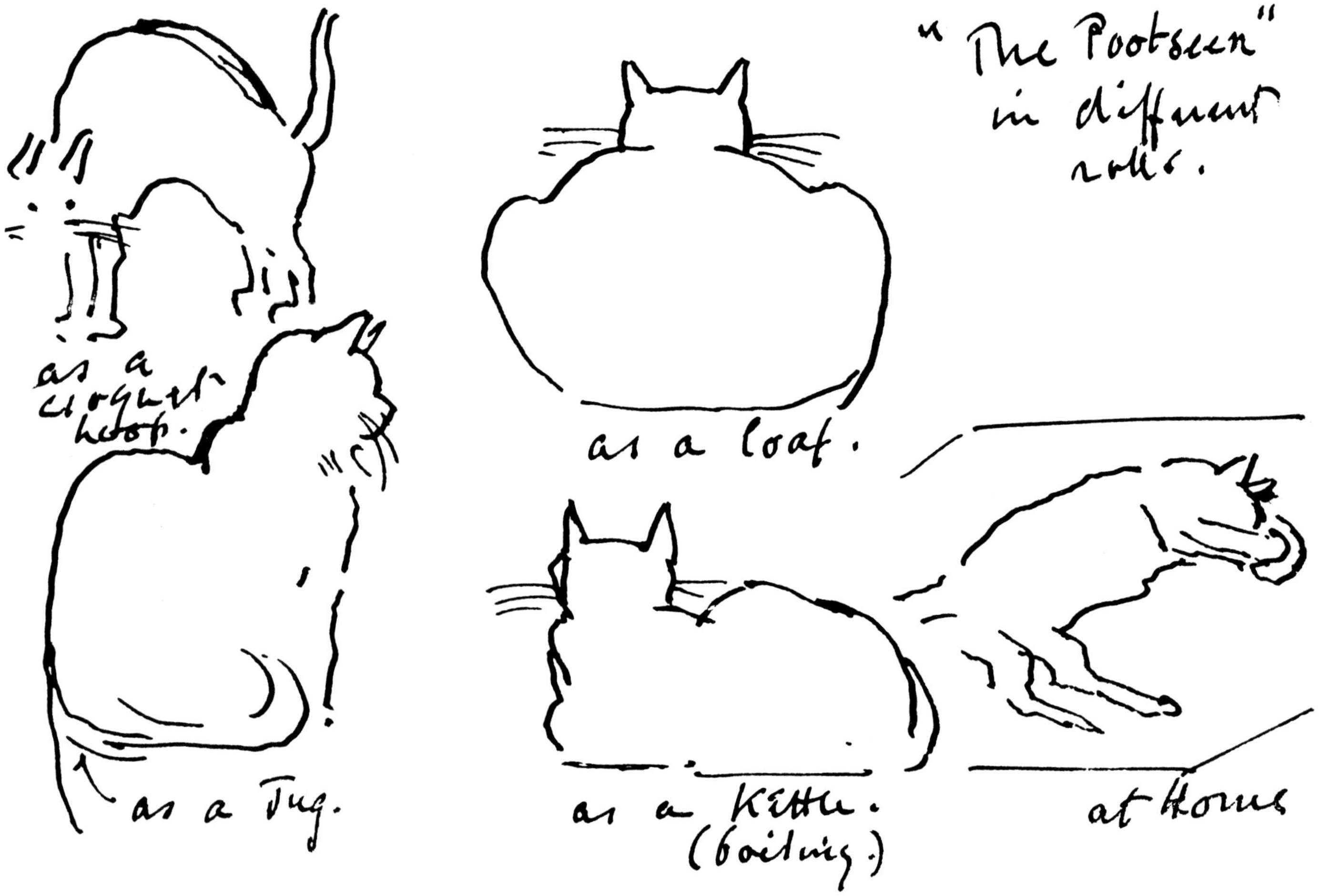
"The Pootseen" in different roles.
as a croquet hoop.
as a loaf.
as a Jug.
as a Kettle. (boiling.)
at Home

Epilogue

Ted Stewart was one of the executors of Bunty's estate. There was relatively little work involved as, apart from a few pieces of furniture and some personal effects, the only assets available comprised the unsold paintings in the studio at 4 Warriston Crescent. Stuart wrote to Jean Perceval-Clark on March 3rd 1938:

"This problem of selling the pictures is certainly a difficult one. I hope that Bunty will come into his own some day and that his pictures will be much more valuable than they are at present. I suppose, however, that this is always what is hoped when an Artist dies. Even if it does happen, we can hardly expect it to happen soon, and I do feel the wisest policy is to sell what we can now when there are certain people who are realising what a loss Bunty is and would like to take a chance of buying something of his when they can. As time passes these people are apt to forget, so I think that when we can get anything like a decent offer, we should accept it".

There is no evidence that any good offers were immediately forthcoming, though some interest must have been generated by the Memorial Exhibition which opened in Edinburgh in April 1942 and then moved to Glasgow in June.

However, for many years most of the interest in Bunty's work and that of his fellow Colourists, Peploe, Hunter and Fergusson has come from within Scotland or from those with Scottish connections. In Bunty's case it is, perhaps, the least surprising as his nationalist spirit and love of life in the comfortable confines of Edinburgh, Glasgow and the Western Isles meant that he had no real desire to move to London, although there is little doubt that, had he chosen to do so, his artistic versatility and personal charisma would have ensured his success.

It is this insularity that is one of the main reasons for the delay in the due international acclaim being accorded to his work. In his book *'Three Scottish Colourists'*, published in 1950, T. J. Honeyman felt that this was relatively unimportant.

". . . it does not matter so very much to us if the Scots to whom we pay tribute fail to become well known outwith their national boundaries. They have given and continue to give delight to thousands and, who knows, they may have blazed a trail for a noble band of successors".

Paintings by the Colourists now have an international following. Exhibitions and auction sales devoted entirely to their work have helped to re-awaken public awareness of four Scottish artists whose paintings hang quite happily in the company of the best British and continental works of the same period. They have now started to command similar prices.

It would have pleased Bunty to have seen his work held in such high regard, but not for mercenary reasons. It would have been enough to have known that others now shared and appreciated his sense of beauty.

Looking back over his career, it is tempting to allow Bunty's forceful and colourful personality to divert one's attention away from his work and overlook the very significant contribution that he made. His pre-occupation with natural beauty and the colour that created it was a major force in helping Scottish painting to shed the stylistic restrictions of the nineteenth century and to lay the foundation of a Colourist tradition that has helped to place twentieth century Scottish artists in the vanguard of the modern European movement.

Plate 88

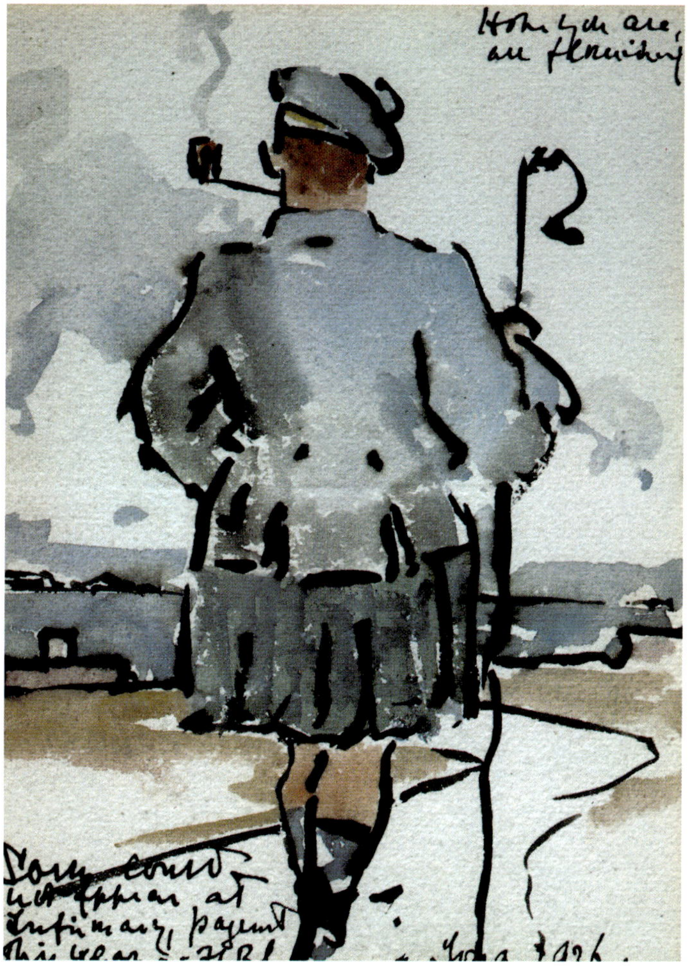

Card from Iona, 1926 watercolour 9 × 6 in.

Exhibitions include:

1908	Edinburgh	Doig, Wilson & Wheatley
1909	Edinburgh	Aitken Dott & Son
1910	Edinburgh	Aitken Dott & Son
1912	Edinburgh	New Gallery: Society of Éight First Exhibition
1917	Glasgow	George Davidson Ltd. (July and November)
1921	Glasgow	Warneuke's Gallery
1922	Glasgow	Warneuke's Gallery
	Edinburgh	Aitken Dott & Son
	Glasgow	Alex. Reid
1923	London	The Leicester Galleries
	Glasgow	Alex. Reid
1924	Glasgow	Alex. Reid
	Paris	Galerie Barbazanges: "Les Peintures de L'Ecosse Moderne"
1925	London	The Leicester Galleries
1926	Glasgow	Alex. Reid
	Dunfermline	Carnegie Dunfermline Trust
1927	Glasgow	Alex. Reid & Lefevre
1928	Glasgow	Alex. Reid & Lefevre
	Kirkcaldy	Museum and Art Gallery
1931	Paris	Galeries Georges Petit: "Les Peintres Ecossais"
	Edinburgh	Parson's Gallery
1932	London	Barbizon House: "Paintings by Six Scottish Artists"
	Edinburgh	Aitken Dott & Son
	Edinburgh	The Scottish Gallery (Aitken Dott & Son)
1933	Glasgow	Pearson & Westergaard
1934	Glasgow	Pearson & Westergaard
	London	Royal Academy: Exhibition of Scottish Art
1938	Glasgow	Palace of Arts: The Empire Exhibition
1939	London	Alex. Reid & Lefevre: "Three Scottish Painters"
	London	Royal Academy: Exhibition of Scottish Art
1942	Edinburgh	National Gallery of Scotland: Cadell Memorial Exhibition
	Glasgow	Glasgow Art Gallery: Cadell Memorial Exhibition
1948	Glasgow	T & R Annan & Sons: "Four Scottish Colourists"
1949	Edinburgh	Royal Scottish Academy: Festival Exhibition
1952	Edinburgh	Aitken Dott & Son: Festival Exhibition
	Edinburgh	Saltire Society: "Four Scottish Colourists"
1970	Scotland	Scottish Arts Council Touring Exhibition: "Three Scottish Colourists"
1971	London	The Fine Art Society: "The Scottish Colourists"
1977	London & Edinburgh	The Fine Art Society: "Three Scottish Colourists"
1983	London & Edinburgh	The Fine Art Society: "F. C. B. Cadell Centenary"
1988	London	Portland Gallery
	Edinburgh	Bourne Fine Art

Plate 89

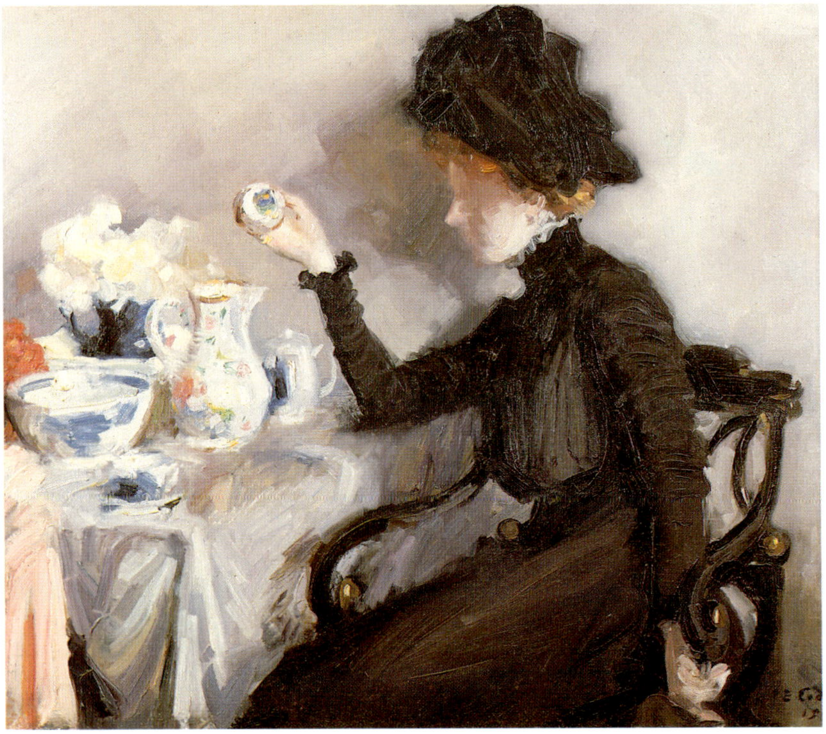

Jean in Black, 1909 oil 24 × 28 in.

Plate 90

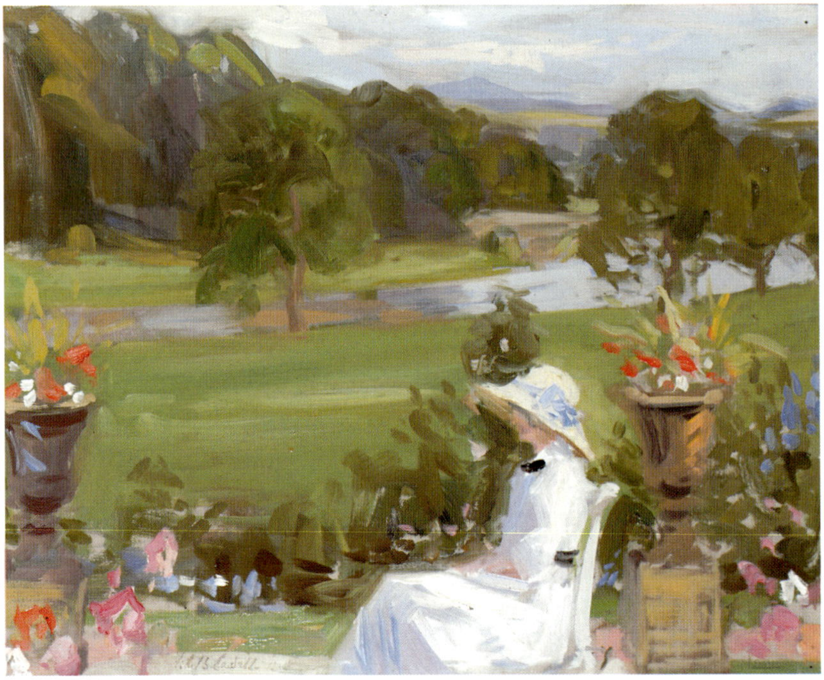

Jean at Dalserf, 1912 oil 15 × 18 in.

Plate 91

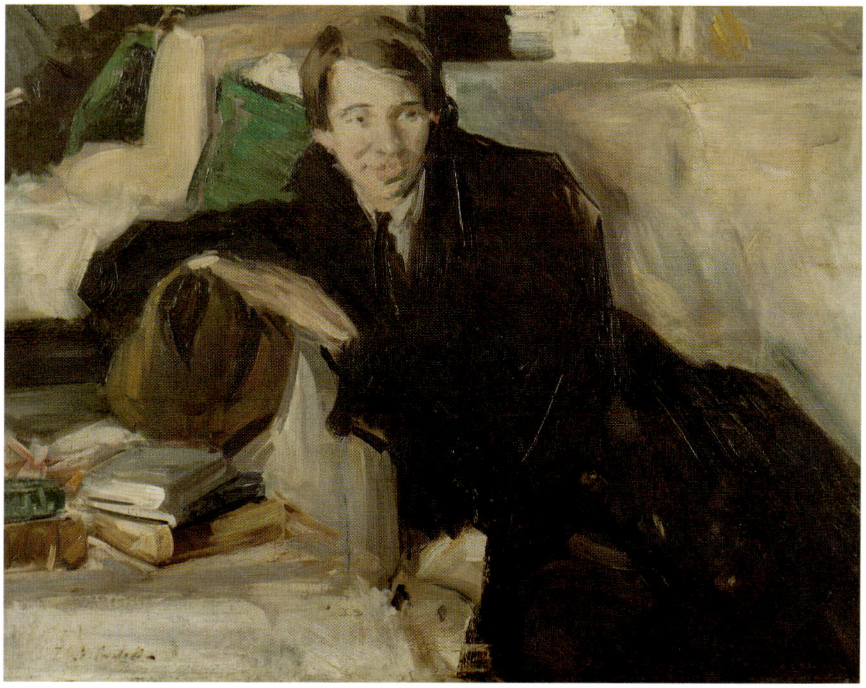

The Poet (R.S.A. Diploma Work)

Plate 92

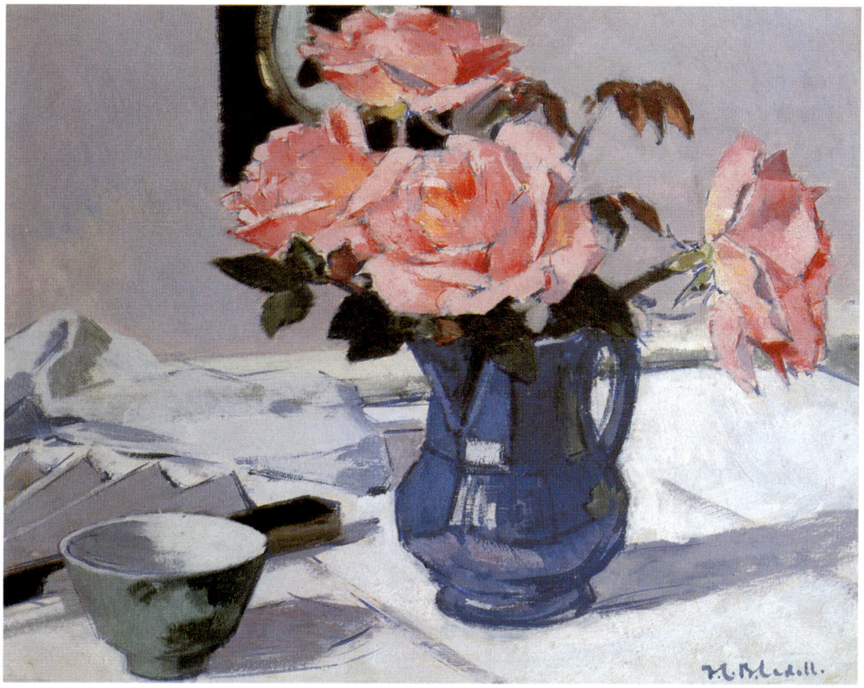

Pink Roses in a Blue Jug, c. 1925 oil 15 × 18 in.

Works Exhibited

Below is a list of works exhibited at the Royal Scottish Academy (R.S.A.), the Royal Glasgow Institute (R.G.I.), and the Royal Scottish Society of Painters in Watercolour (R.S.W.).

1902	Portrait	R.S.A.
	Notre Dame from the Seine	R.S.A.
1904	Old Houses, Inverkeithing, Fife	R.S.A.
1905	Old Doorway, Inverkeithing	R.S.A.
1907	Schloss Gassa, Gotha	R.S.A.
1909	Paris Street	R.G.I.
1911	Henry Johnstone Esq.	R.S.A.
	Interior	R.G.I.
1912	Lady in Black	R.S.A.
	The Mirror	R.S.A.
1913	The Blue Dress	R.S.A.
	Interior	R.S.A.
	Girl in a Ballet Dress	R.G.I.
	China and Glass	R.G.I.
1914	Timothy Inkpen	R.S.A.
	Herman at the Mantlepiece	R.G.I.
1915	Interior with Figure	R.S.A.
	Morning	R.S.A.
	Afternoon	R.S.A.
	Crème de Menthe	R.G.I.
	Reflection	R.G.I.
1916	The Poet	R.S.A.
	A Person of Importance	R.S.A.
	In the Park	R.S.A.
	Interior with Figure	R.G.I.
	Objects	R.G.I.
	Lady with a Black Hat	R.G.I.
1917	At the Mantlepiece	R.S.A.
	Interior	R.S.A.
	Reflection	R.S.A.
	Afternoon	R.G.I.
	At the Mirror	R.G.I.
	The Fawn Dress	R.G.I.
1918	The Mirror	R.S.A.
	J. G. Jardine-Binnie Esq.	R.S.A.
	The Fireplace in Summer	R.G.I.
1919	Portrait of a Girl	R.S.A.
	Interior	R.S.A.
	Still Life	R.S.A.
	Poisonous Gas	R.S.A.
	The Opera	R.S.A.
	The Tired Horse	R.S.A.
	The Footballer	R.S.A.
	Carnations	R.G.I.
	Tulips	R.G.I.
1920	Reflection	R.G.I.
	Roses	R.G.I.
1921	Negro with Orange	R.S.A.
	Still Life	R.S.A.
	The Country House	R.S.A.
	Interior	R.G.I.
	The Buddha (Black and gold)	R.G.I.
	Portrait of a Lady In Black	R.G.I.
1922	The Negro and the Orange	R.G.I.
	Interior	R.G.I.
	Embroidered Cloak	R.G.I.
1923	Lady in Black and Gold	R.G.I.
1924	Landscape	R.G.I.
	Interior	R.G.I.
	The White Villa	R.G.I.
1925	Nigger in White	R.S.A.
	Iona – looking East	R.G.I.
	Interior	R.G.I.
	Village, Iona	R.G.I.
1926	Study (pencil & wash)	R.S.A.
	Girl with a Fan	R.G.I.
	A Lady in Black	R.G.I.
	Lunga from Iona	R.G.I.
1927	Still Life – Anemones	R.G.I.
	The Faun Dress – Interior with a Figure	R.G.I.
	Foyer de thêatre	R.G.I.
1928	Cattle on the Shore, Iona	R.G.I.
	Interior – the Orange Blind	R.G.I.
1929	Cattle on the Shore	R.S.A.
	Interior – the Red Chair	R.S.A.
	Roses	R.S.A.
	Open Window	R.G.I.
	Interior – Summer	R.G.I.
	Landscape – the West Highlands	R.G.I.
1930	Interior – the Eagle Mirror	R.S.A.
	Interior	R.S.A.
	Interior	R.G.I.
	Still Life	R.G.I.
	Still Life	R.G.I.
1931	Ben More	R.S.A.
	A Lady in Black and Gold	R.S.A.
	Interior	R.S.A.
	Santa Maria della Salute, Venice	R.G.I.
	The Castle	R.G.I.
	Auchnacraig	R.G.I.

1932	Interior	R.S.A.
	Still Life	R.S.A.
	Santa Maria della Salute, Venice	R.S.A.
	Marigolds	R.G.I.
	The Jesuati, Venice	R.G.I.
	Iona – the Village	R.G.I.
1933	Interior	R.S.A.
	Iona	R.S.A.
	The Castle	R.S.A.
	Negro's Head	R.S.A.
	Drawing	R.S.A.
	The Proprietor	R.S.A.
	Interior	R.G.I.
	G. W. Service, Esq.	R.G.I.
	Cottage Interior	R.G.I.
1934	The Road to the Village	R.S.A.
	Black and Gold	R.S.A.
	Pink Carnations	R.S.A.
	Changing Edinburgh	R.S.A.
	Arrivals – The Opera	R.S.A.
	Their Graces	R.S.A.
	The Poet	R.G.I.
	Interior	R.G.I.
	Interior	R.G.I.
1935	Rocks	R.S.A.
	The Poet	R.S.A.
	Aloes	R.S.A.
	Glengarry	R.S.A.
	A Minor Incident in the Great War	R.S.A.
	The Wink	R.S.A.
	Portrait of a Lady	R.G.I.
	Ben More, in Mull	R.G.I.
	Sea Avenue	R.G.I.
	An Iona Croft	R.S.W.
	A Paris Street	R.S.W.
	Cassis	R.S.W.
	Summer in Iona	R.S.W.
1936	Mrs Christopher Guest	R.S.A.
	Still Life	R.S.A.
	Boats – Venice	R.S.A.
	Drawing	R.S.A.
	The Country House	R.S.A.
	Inverary	R.S.A.
	The Grey Bowler	R.G.I.
	Interior – Regent Terrace	R.G.I.
	Roses	R.G.I.
	Venus and Adonis	R.S.W.
	Arrivals – The Opera	R.S.W.
	Their Graces	R.S.W.
	Dennis	R.S.W.
1937	Still Life – Azalea	R.S.A.
	A Castle in Argyll	R.S.A.
	Interior – the Blue Room	R.S.A.
1938	The Eagle Mirror	R.S.A.
	The Mirror	R.S.A.
	Venice – Grand Canal	R.S.A.
	The White Sofa	R.S.A.
1947	Iona Landscape	R.S.A.
1976	The White Room	R.S.A.

Plate 93

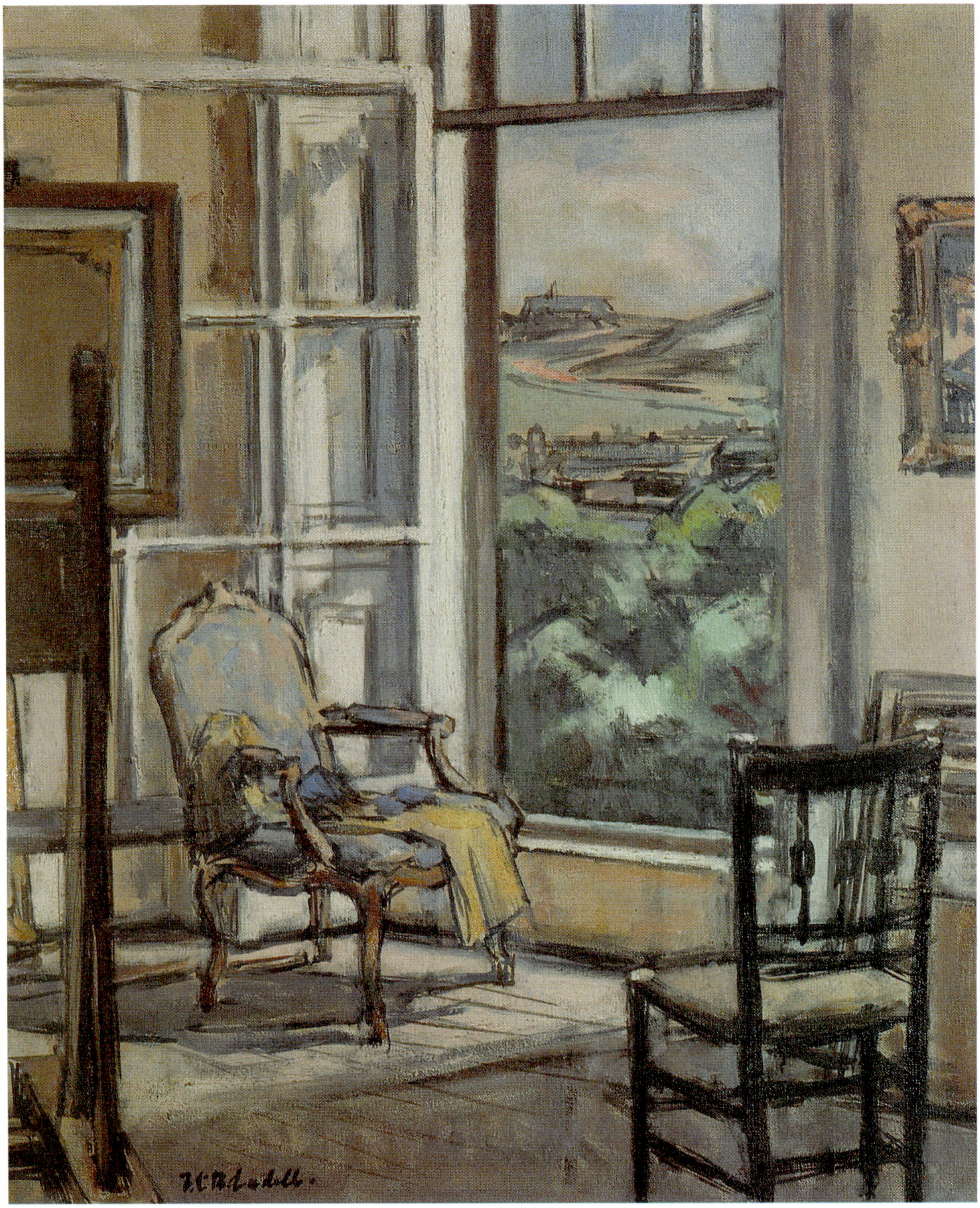

The Open Window, 1933 oil 24 × 20 in.

Plate 94

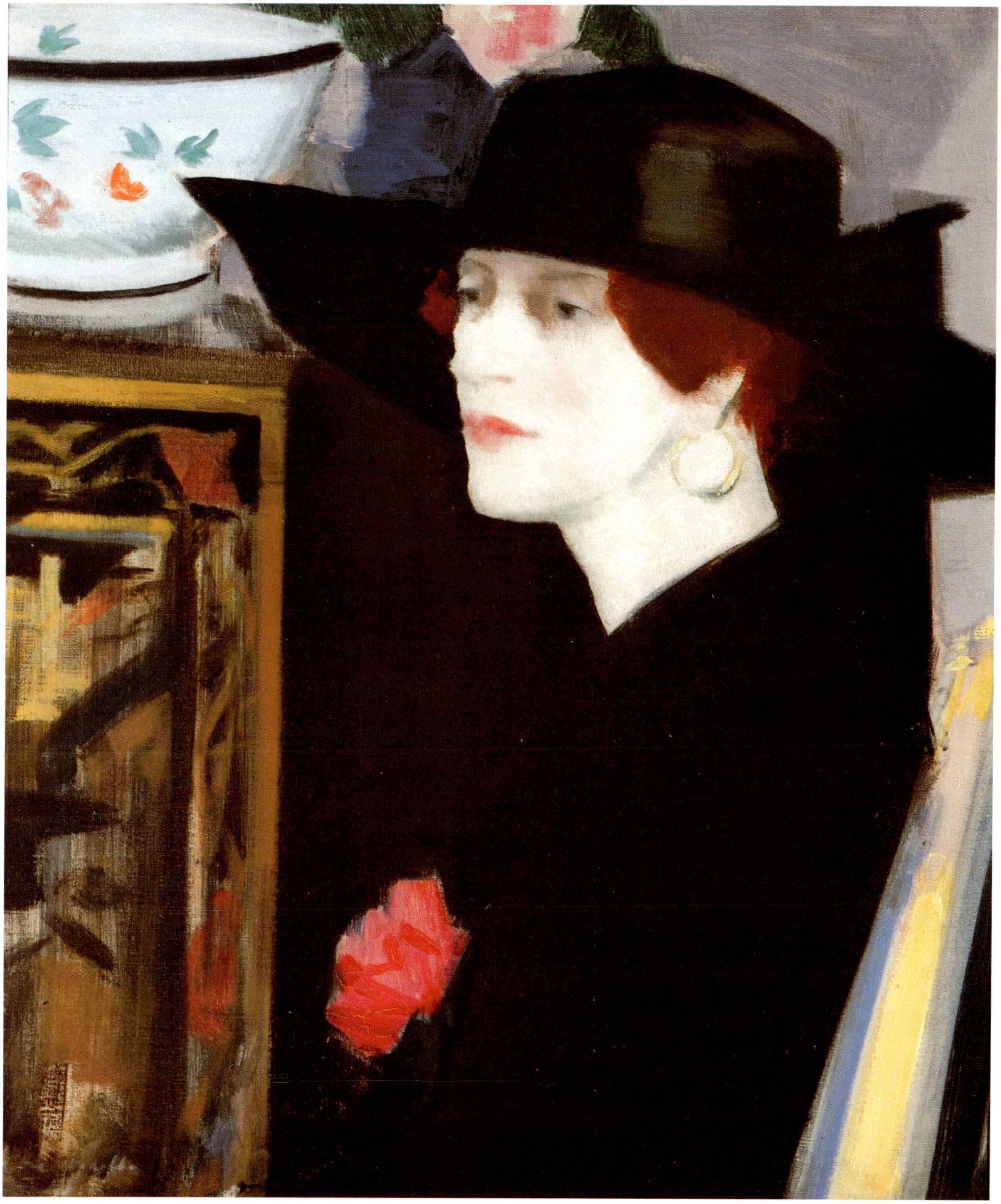

Lady in a Black Hat, c. 1926 oil 24 × 20 in.

Bibliography

Billcliffe, R.	The Glasgow Boys, London 1985
Cursiter, S.	Peploe, London 1947
Hardie, W.	Scottish Painting 1837-1839, London 1976
Honeyman, T. J.	Three Scottish Colourists, London 1950
Morris, M.	The Art of J. D. Fergusson, Glasgow 1974
Peploe, G.	F. C. B. Cadell, A Critical Memoir

Exhibition Catalogues and Periodicals:

Glasgow Art Gallery, Cadell Memorial Exhibition, June 1942.
Introduction by Stanley Cursiter.

Scottish Arts Council Exhibition Catalogue, 'Three Scottish Colourists', 1970.

Guildford House Gallery Exhibition Catalogue, 'Three Scottish Colourists', 1980.

Studio Magazine: 1913 Volume LVII
1914 Volume LXI
1916 Volume LXVII
1923 Volume LXXXVI
1932 Volume CIV

Apollo Magazine: 1931 Volume XIII
1939 Volume XXIX

Connoisseur Magazine: 1913 Volume XXXIV

Plate 95

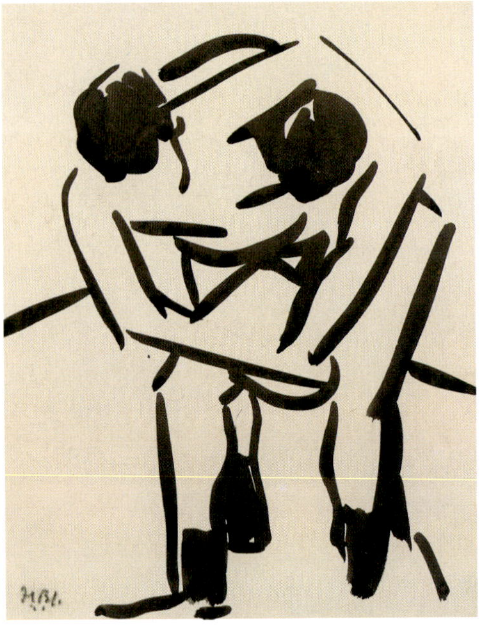

Wrestlers, 1912 14 × 10 in.

Index

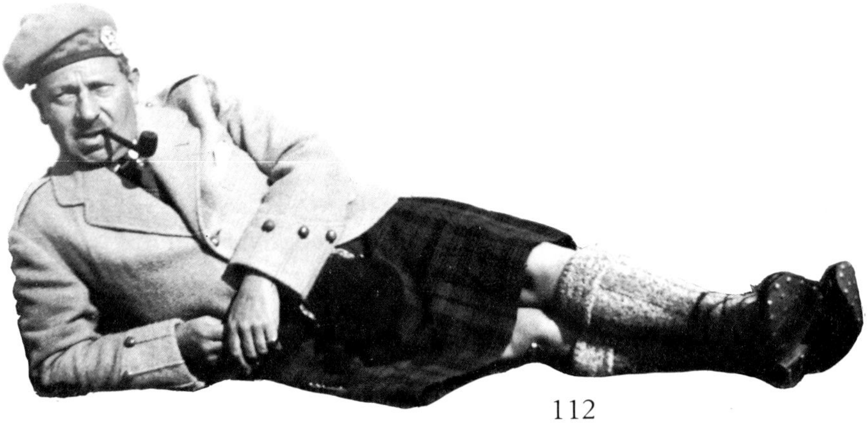